80 QUESTIONS FOR ADOLESCENTS

A GUIDE TO MAKING SENSE OF SCHOOL AND LIFE

By

Derek J. Lovett

This book was created in partnership with *Put Student Motivation First,* a 501(c)(3) focused on increasing academic motivation among middle and high school students (www.psmfnow.org).

This book was edited by Margaret A. Lovett.

The book cover was designed by Chris Hardy (www.chrishardy.co).

TABLE OF CONTENTS

A NOTE TO PARENTS & TEACHERS

This book is broken down into three distinct modules, each with five chapters. Each chapter encompasses a narrative followed by thought-provoking questions meant to spur self-reflection and analysis.

Topic 1: Why Are You Here?

In this section students will be challenged to think critically about school and the role it plays in their vision, goals, and success.

Topic 2: Who's Coming with You?

In this section students will be challenged to consider positive and negative influences, as well as responsibility to self, family, and community.

Topic 3: What Will You Do?

In this section students will be challenged to evaluate their shortcomings, develop a plan of action, and set measurable goals.

A MESSAGE TO STUDENTS

Believe it or not, when I was in school, I felt much like you probably do about it. I was bored with it. I did not see the real point of it all. After the 7th grade, I was never the most focused or committed student. Most of my high school and college years were plagued by procrastination and a half-hearted effort. Aiding my bad habits in high school was the fact that I could make A's with ease. Yet, many times I still felt so unmotivated.

So, if you are asking yourself why you must read another book then I will just tell you this: This book really is for you. I did not write it from the perspective of, "I did this, and you should too." Instead, I wrote it from the perspective of, "I did this, and here is what I learned from it. While I have been fortunate enough to have some success in this life, I know that I have left a lot of potential on the table.

I have learned a lot on my journey. My thoughts, reflections, and lessons learned are what I am sharing with you. Fortunately, I have had a strong enough support system to push me forward even when I have wanted to quit. Because of this I can now see how my errors could have been devastating if I had not had that support. Maybe you have a great support system like I did. Or maybe you do not. And maybe you feel like you are slowly losing hope and are on the verge of dropping out of school or just giving up on life. If that is you, I want to encourage you to hang in there!

No matter how you feel right now, I can almost guarantee that your feelings are quite natural and nothing that is uncommon to the many individuals who are undergoing similar circumstances. So, while you may feel alone at times, know that you are not alone. But here is what I want you to understand right now: You are at a critical juncture in your life where your decisions can either put you on a trajectory of success or failure. Many times, this comes with much discomfort and uncertainty. And it is how you respond to these things that will determine what you will become as well as the type of work you will do for the rest of your life. The beauty in all of this is that you have the power to develop the life you want!

If you begin making decisions now that are based on the future you want, then it will dynamically change your life and the lives of those around you. My hope is that by reading this book you will broaden your perspective of the world around you, as well as develop a greater sense of purpose for your life, so you can better make those decisions. Consider this your wake-up call. Rise and shine!

TOPIC 1: WHY ARE YOU HERE?

CHAPTER 1—KNOWING WHAT YOU WANT

Self-awareness

What do you want out of life? While this question may seem simple, it is probably one of the toughest questions for most people to answer. While deep down we all have an idea of what we want, life has a way of cluttering the mind and causing confusion. Therefore, many people right now are living lives that someone else designed for them and are not pursuing what they truly want.

Have you ever had a craving for a certain food? In that moment, you knew that only that food would "hit the spot" and nothing else would suffice. Well, in the same way, you must know what you want out of life so that you won't settle for less. Ironically, 20 or 30 years from now when you can look back on your life and see the "big picture," the things that stopped you from what you wanted will seem small and insignificant. However, right now many of these things probably seem overwhelmingly significant. Therefore, in this book we will attempt to define what these obstacles are and how they can negatively affect your quest to achieve the life you want. By doing so you will be better equipped to deal with them.

When a person determines what they really want out of life it guides everything they do. "Knowing what you want" and "thinking about what you might want" are two vastly different things. "Knowing what you want" implies a confidence that the other does not. Consider the following analogy: Have you ever misplaced something and then quickly looked in the places you knew it had to be but could not find it? Then it was not until you finally decided to take your time and look thoroughly enough to begin eliminating some of the options that you found it. So, what changed from the first time? The second time you looked with a greater intent and purpose that grew as you eliminated the other possibilities. In the same way, knowing what you want will empower you to stay focused and driven.

I want to tell you a quick story. As I sat in my engineering orientation class my first year of college at Tennessee State University, the Dean of the College of Engineering emphatically stated that 2 out of every 3 students in the class would not finish the engineering program. Immediately, we all looked around as to say, "It's not going to be me!" Yet, sure enough, my dean was right. The ratio of students in that room that did not make it through the engineering program turned out to be even greater than 2 out of every 3. Of course, every student that did not make it had their own reason—some found another interest, some felt it was too difficult, and others just did not do what was necessary to pass. Nonetheless, my dean understood something that many of us did not quite yet—he knew that our success would take more than desire.

While none of us wanted to be counted out, the truth of the matter was that we were all about to be tested to see if what we professed was what we really wanted. At this point, we were all under the presumption that we were there to get an engineering degree. However, for most of us— if we were honest with ourselves— we would have thought otherwise. That same class period my dean posed a challenge to us that, in reflecting over the years, has grown in significance for me. He asked us to write down our 3 and 5-year goals. At that time in my life, I had never really considered what I genuinely wanted out of life. I was 17! I knew the basic things that were popular— a nice home, a good paying job, and a nice car— so that is what I wrote down. Yet, I struggled to find anything I could truly make an emotional connection with. If I had really understood the importance of that exercise, I would have recognized that I did not want to be an engineer! At the time I wanted to pursue Broadcast Journalism. I loved to write and loved the idea of performing in front of a camera. It just so happened that I was choosing to do engineering for all the wrong reasons—pressures from loved ones, influences of society, and foolish pride!

It would be years later before I realized that this moment was the beginning of an important lesson for me. I had to learn to define success for myself and not allow it to be defined by other people's ideas of success. In retrospect, I applaud those that realized engineering was not for them and chose to do something they felt they either enjoyed more or were better equipped for. I graduated with an engineering degree, but my college experience was a lot more strenuous than it had to be. While the engineering program posed its own set of challenges, my most formidable challenge was a lack of motivation.

Diligence

My lack of motivation quickly became evident in my actions throughout my first year and lasted for several years after that. Foremost, I developed a terrible habit of not doing homework. During my first year, I would return to my dorm after classes knowing that I needed to do homework—and many times would even desire to do it—but instead would lay in bed watching television. On the occasions that I mustered up the fortitude to try to do my homework, I usually ended up staring at the wall or through the window for hours. The reality was that, although I knew what was necessary, I still did not have any real motivation. I did not know what I wanted, and it showed! I ended up losing my scholarship after that first semester.

Does any of this sound familiar to you? Whether it does or not, I have some good news. You have an opportunity right now to define what you want so that you can move aggressively in the direction of it. Once you define what you want you can start the process of defining the necessary steps to get there. As you gain clarity about what you want this process becomes even easier. While this process will continue for the rest of your life, you can start making it work for you now. To develop a solid foundation for this, we will focus on 3 things throughout this book: 1.) Vision, 2.) Goals, and 3.) Boundaries.

We will define vision as "the state, or condition, of knowing what you want." For simplification, you can think of it simply as "what you want out of life." Furthermore, goals are "the steps you take to get to your vision." When individuals try to set goals that are not based on their vision they tend to get tired and discouraged, just like I did my first year of college. Therefore, you must first define a vision to know what goals to set. As you make progress, it will also become easier to identify the things that do not belong. Finally, to avoid those things that do not belong you must establish certain rules, or "boundaries," that will not allow you to compromise on the things you know you should or should not be doing. You can think of boundaries like the out-of-bounds lines on a basketball court—crossing them at the wrong time turns the ball over to the other team. In the same way, when you overstep these boundaries, it will impede your progress.

You are at a juncture in your life in which it is integral for you to implement these three aspects so that you can stay focused and diligent in the pursuit of what you want. Even with a strong desire, without these things you will inevitably begin making decisions that take you away from your desired path. An adage you may be familiar with states, "If you don't stand for something then you will fall for anything." Have you heard this before? This is so true! Not establishing a vision, nor subsequent goals or boundaries, will leave you vulnerable to momentary distractions that may be contrary to your progress. This is how a lot of people get into trouble. While they may not have a real desire for the

"If you don't stand for something then you will fall for anything."

things that distract them, the mistakes they make while being distracted sometimes have far-reaching consequences!

Through the course of this text, you will have an opportunity to establish a vision and set goals and boundaries that will help you hold fast to that vision. In preparation for that, I encourage you to start thinking about what you want out of life. So, what does success look like for you right now? Can school have an important part to play in it? If you do not see school as an opportunity to help you achieve what you want, then naturally you will struggle to be motivated. However, if you can see it helping you then you can find motivation to succeed. Here is my proposal to you: Since right now you have chosen to continue attending school, make the most of the opportunity! As you define what you want, school can become much more than just a place where you are forced to go to classes you don't care about—it can become a place you desire to be because of the benefits it can provide to helping you achieve your vision.

SELF-REFLECTION

1. What do you want to do as a career?

2. What is your idea of a successful life?

3. What influences have shaped your outlook of success?

CHAPTER 2—BELIEVING YOU CAN ACHIEVE

Courage

What do you believe you can achieve? I will make this simple for you. If I really wanted to know what you believed, I would simply look at what your actions told me. While we all may have moments that aren't reflective of our character, the patterns of our lives tell a story. Therefore, if you truly believe you can be successful in school then that success should be evident in your behavior. Likewise, if you told me you were destined to have a certain career, then I would expect to see you making progress towards that career on a daily basis. If you truly believe in something, then you will find a way to make it happen. Therefore, a lack of progress is indicative of a lack of belief. Many people simply don't believe what they say they believe, and that's why they are not moving in that direction.

Let me further clarify how we can identify belief. There's one thing about belief that I know—when a person truly believes in something they have a passion for it. And passion will not let you be stagnant. It forces you to act! Belief is always evident in some form or fashion. Yes, it is also important to note that belief can be developed. Forming a belief is a process. Whether you realize it or not, you are forming beliefs every day. Therefore, every individual is constantly building towards something, either a life of fulfillment or a life that lacks purpose and substance. Naturally, we all desire fulfillment. However, deterrents such as fear, doubt, discouragement, and insecurity are obstacles to belief that tend to cause individuals to veer off their desired path. Therefore, if you believe you can achieve something then you must prepare to take those obstacles head on. If you do not, then you will struggle to make progress towards the life you truly want.

So, what do you believe you can achieve? Rather, do you believe that you can have what you want? Believe it or not, your belief determines your capacity for carrying out your vision. Now that you have begun determining your vision, it is important that you understand how to form the beliefs that will help you move forward. Belief is basically a product of two things: 1.) your thoughts and 2.) your actions. It is an accepted truth that continuing to think about something, whether good or bad, eventually becomes a reality in the mind. That is, we will begin to believe whatever we dwell on. Furthermore, our actions reinforce what we believe. While acting towards your vision is an outward indication to others of your belief, it also serves to reaffirm your personal belief. Therefore, acting on your vision is for you more than anyone else! Conversely, not acting on your vision can (and will) weaken your belief over time.

Prudence

Many people talk themselves out of what they truly want because they never build up the gumption to act on it. Therefore, over time they subscribe to another belief, and what was once a clear and uncompromising vision becomes marred with conditions. "Well, if it doesn't happen then it is just not for me," you've probably heard individuals say. While this is true in some cases, many times individuals use statements like this to detract from their own responsibility in manifesting the vision they have for their life. I am sure that I've said something like this at times in my life about something I really wanted. Maybe you have done the same. While there are some cases in which our aspirations may be "somewhere in left field," many times we are just lacking belief because somewhere down the line we have failed to take the necessary actions to continue to ignite that belief.

For a moment, consider how your thoughts and actions may have created some beliefs in your life. Inevitably, you will have some that are both good and bad. The reality is that every day, through establishing the right thoughts and actions, you have an opportunity to construct beliefs that support your vision. In this regard, it is important right now that you recognize the patterns that may be forming beliefs that are counterproductive to your vision.

So, how can you actively establish the right beliefs? Foremost, you must understand how your environment affects your beliefs. Your thoughts stem from how you are influenced. That is, what you see, hear, and feel is what shapes your view of the world and how you see yourself in it.

Therefore, in terms of your belief, you are constantly being influenced positively or negatively.

Let's consider a couple of scenarios. An individual who is exposed to a negative environment for an extended period—such as one in which he or she is a victim of some type of abuse and has no clear-cut path of relief—may eventually succumb to discouragement. Naturally, they may then resort to self-pity which can lead to certain behaviors that are counterproductive to personal growth and development. In this case a negative influence creates negative thoughts that bring about negative beliefs and, finally, negative actions. This cycle of negativity might continue if that individual's circumstances don't change. On the other hand, if that same individual is exposed to a positive environment for an extended period—such as one in which he or she is constantly uplifted and encouraged—this will naturally help reinforce self-esteem. Likely, that individual will begin to adopt an optimism about life that can lead to beliefs and actions that align with what he or she wants.

While every individual has their own unique set of circumstances, the bottom line is that influences either make it harder or easier to embrace the positive thinking that is needed to move in the direction of what you want to achieve in life. Knowing this, it is in your best interest to reduce your exposure to negative environments as much as possible. While you may not be able to control some of your environments, such as where you live or attend school, you can be strategic with what you can control. For instance, while an individual may be the constant target of verbal assaults, he or she may have to use every opportunity possible to listen to positive, uplifting music or podcasts that help them remember what they are striving for.

Believe it or not, many individuals become the biggest hindrance to their own lives. Let me explain. Negative thought patterns that hinder belief in oneself can easily become the result of many disappointments. While this is naturally not anyone's intention, it is a sheer reality. To circumvent these patterns, we must first identify them. Right now, take a moment to consider how your self-image may have been affected by positive and negative environments over the years. Can you see a pattern in your thoughts and actions due to any of your experiences or circumstances? Did you use to believe you could achieve certain things but now you struggle to find that same passion and zeal? Whatever your observations are, know that right now you have exactly what you need to ignite your belief and move in the direction of your vision.

SELF-REFLECTION

4. Do you have someone that you look up to? Who is it and what makes them special to you?

5. Who are the most successful people you know?

6. What characteristics make them successful? How has this person influenced you?

7. Do you believe you can be as successful? Why or why not?

8. What are you currently doing to achieve success?

CHAPTER 3—THE PURPOSE OF SCHOOL

Perspective

Do you think school is important? This is a question I like to pose to students. Most answer with, "Yes, of course!" However, they tend to have a tough time explaining to me why they gave that answer. They may say that it is important "To get a job" or "To get an education," but most can't go any further than that. While there are no right or wrong answers for this, the reality is that if you don't define what you truly value about school then it doesn't matter what anyone else tells you about its importance. Just like I struggled with motivation my freshman year of college, you will have a tough time being motivated if you can't identify how school is helping you achieve what you want for your life. Furthermore, just as only you can define your vision, only you can define why school is important to you.

Right now, many students see school as an obligation and not a privilege. While you may have some criticisms of school, I want to challenge you to see some of its positive aspects. To begin, my question to you is: Do you feel that your time could be better spent doing something other than attending school? If you answered "Yes," then my next question is this: How would you spend that time? If you feel that you could be using your time better elsewhere then surely you have a thorough plan in mind for how you would go about your day, right? Or maybe not? Before you make up your mind about what school has to offer, it is beneficial that you identify what school really is and what it can be for you.

Foremost, school provides you with the structure needed to learn and develop as a person. For a moment, consider what you would be doing if you were at home and could spend your time in any way you wanted. This past summer, if you were not in some type of camp, or working, then you probably have some good examples of what might happen. Did you work studiously to improve your academics or learn about your future career? For a few students that may have been the case, but for most students it was not. This type of development typically requires the structure that school provides.

Without school you likely would not take the necessary steps to develop the skills you need to be a functional and contributing member of society. Whether you know it or not, there are millions of young people right now in the world living in utter poverty that don't have the opportunity to attain a formal education. As a result, many of them will die prematurely in poverty or resort to a life of crime to survive. While you may have criticisms about the way things are done at your school, the bottom line is that you still are able to attend school and benefit from teachers, counselors, and peers. No matter what you want to do—whether it is owning a business or simply learning how to provide for your family— school can provide the foundation, if you allow it to.

In contrast to the volatility of the outside world, school is meant to be a controlled environment where help is readily available. Furthermore, contrary to popular belief, those in authority are not there to make your life miserable. While you may not be comfortable approaching everyone for help, it is likely you can find a staff member that will be willing to take you under their wing and give you some guidance. Furthermore, while teachers are there as facilitators, you are of the age at which you can make definitive decisions for the improvement of your own life. School is an opportunity to learn the skills you need to take care of you and your family while building the life you want. Therefore, it is your responsibility to take learning into your own hands.

SELF-REFLECTION

9. Why do you come to school?

10. Could you survive in the real world on your own right now? Why or why not?

11. What is your opinion of how school prepares students for life?

12. Are you taking full advantage of the structure it provides?

13. What steps can you take to make the most out of this opportunity?

CHAPTER 4—EVALUATING INTERESTS & GOALS

Self-awareness

For a moment, I want you to reflect on the foundation we're building. So far, we've gone over what you want, what you believe, and why you should view school as a resource for helping you move your life in the direction that you want it to go. Now it's time to establish your interests and goals. This will help bring perspective to everything else. To start, let's consider the idea of having a career. Evolving technologies have created a growing pool of career opportunities for those who are willing to do the legwork. These opportunities look much different than they did 20 years ago. For instance, the advent of digital marketing has enabled individuals with average skill sets to leverage carefully crafted marketing strategies into multi-million-dollar brands. Moreover, individuals who can develop a high proficiency in niche markets such as print-on-demand apparel or results coaching can generate just as much income as those who excel in traditional academic fields such as law and medicine. So, what does this mean for you? It means that there are many options to choose from to help get you where you want to go! But first you must choose.

You can think of a career as a vehicle for bringing that dream to pass. You, as the driver, get to steer that vehicle in the direction of your vision by setting some goals. As you actively do this, you will begin to establish your true interests and gain clarity for how they relate to your vision.

You may remember our earlier discussion about how passion follows whatever you believe. Well, one test when evaluating an interest should be to observe if that interest generates a sense of passion. After all, you must believe in your interests even if no one else does. Even though your interests may change, this is a starting point.

Typically, if you are truly interested in something then you will notice a pattern in your life that exhibits characteristics that align with that interest. That is, there should be some evidence of your interest in the things that you think about and do. Long before I ever wrote my first book, writing was my favorite hobby. Without thinking about it, I would creatively write out my thoughts and reflections imagining that I had an audience either listening or reading. Notebooks that I designated for other uses always ended up being filled with these expressions. While I struggled to be motivated in engineering during my freshman year of college, the highlight of my day was the time I designated in my evenings to write in my journal about that day. I was always writing!

Regrettably, at the time I started college I was so blinded by trying to "prove" that I could do engineering that I didn't realize I was missing out on something that my heart truly desired. Because you are reading this right now, you can make a conscious effort to look critically at the patterns in your life that point towards your true interests. Therefore, if you are serious about figuring this out then this is the time to be real with yourself. You must ask yourself, "What can I see myself doing for a living?" Once you identify this, you can use it to motivate you!

Goal-setting

If you are out to "prove" something, make sure you are doing it because you know it is the best thing for you. That is, make sure it is something you value for yourself and are not doing just for other people. Right now, you may not be sure what you are interested in. That's okay. Many students I have asked over the years about their career interests have replied with, "I don't know." Hopefully, this will become clearer as you continue to reflect. Chances are that even now you have some clue as to your interests and you just need to dig a little deeper. But there is one surefire way to test your interests—you must set some goals!

As I alluded to earlier, one of the keys to experiencing success—and minimizing regrets—is to establish a vision and determine that you will overcome any obstacles that arise as you move in that direction. Having goals provides the structure needed to develop the thoughts and actions necessary to keep moving forward. When you set goals that are aligned with your vision you give yourself leverage to overcome obstacles that under normal circumstances would halt your progress. The key is that you must find the right goals for you and determine that you will accomplish them.

So, how do you establish the right goals? Well, there is no perfect way of doing this. In fact, there are many variations of goals that can be used to manifest your vision. However, the following are three questions you can ask yourself to decide if a goal is right for you:

- Does it align with my vision?
- Do I believe I can achieve it?
- Am I willing to commit to it?

Naturally, your goals should align with your vision, and since every goal has a unique process—and there likely will be setbacks—you must also believe that your goal is attainable! In addition, assessing your interests and talents can help you evaluate if your goal is something that is worth lending your time to. Finally, your commitment is an indicator that you are willing to develop the necessary skills to accomplish your goal.

For clarity, let's briefly define skills and talents. A skill is an attribute that is commonly identifiable as something that can be used to produce a desired result. Your skills are what employers typically look at when they are choosing an ideal candidate for a position. Common examples of skills are "typing" and "use of proper grammar." On the other hand, talent is a knack for executing an action or behavior exceptionally above average. While a skill can be taught, a talent cannot. A talent must simply be identified and then honed. For instance, a skilled public speaker may notice that they have a talent for captivating audiences.

Commitment

Every goal should (1) have a benchmark or deadline, (2) alter your routine or behavior, and (3) have an anticipated, measurable impact on your life. The significance of this is that these three criteria will allow you to measure progress. Keep in mind that, while every goal should contribute to achieving your vision, the goal itself might not be desirable. For instance, someone that desires to be a doctor may not want to go to school for 10 - 14 years after graduating high school but, if that is truly what they want then they must be willing to endure the process.

If your goals don't meet the specified criteria, then you will likely be wasting time pursuing something you either don't truly want or something you will not follow through with. As alluded to earlier, when I started college I didn't understand this concept. If I had, then I would have chosen to major in broadcast journalism. That's where my interest was, I was passionate about it, and I could see myself working in that career field. However, I chose to major in engineering for reasons other than the specified criteria. Ironically enough, I did not envision myself working as an engineer.

When choosing goals, it is extremely important that you define a standard of success for yourself in lieu of what society, or others, may try to establish for you. You should be able to genuinely express why you are doing what you are doing. If you cannot do this, then that is a key indication that you should reevaluate your interests and motives. While there were several factors in my decision to pursue engineering, one of them was the prestige that I felt was associated with it. But that was my childish pride! In retrospect, I realize that I chose an "idea" of success in lieu of defining my own success.

As you consider your goals, keep in mind that they don't have to be elaborate. If they meet the specified criteria, then they can be short and simple. You will see that with each goal you accomplish you are paving the way to your vision. Let's look at an example. An individual aspiring to be a professional singer decides to set a goal of winning a talent show. Furthermore, he or she is committed to competing in talent shows until they win. In this regard, no matter how well this individual performs at each talent show—good or bad—with each performance he or she will gain experience and exposure and will be able to measure progress.

As this individual continues to compete, he or she will better understand the areas they excel in and the ones they need to improve upon. That individual might also discover what he or she most enjoys about singing and, thereby, may be able to better define their vision. For instance, through competing this individual might realize that he or she enjoys musical theatre much more than the idea of being a recording artist. With this discovery, he or she might then set goals that support this, such as a goal of starring in a touring musical production or getting accepted into a reputable university theatre arts program.

Productivity

The main function of your goals is to help you make progress towards your vision. Just as the aspiring singer, the more you move forward with your goals the clearer your vision will become. Therefore, you will either become more assured of what you want, or you will determine that it is no longer what you want. In this regard, even your failures are a win-win! If the individual interested in singing never took the step of entering competitions—or utilizing another outlet for honing their talent—then he or she would likely not have made progress and would have been setting him or herself up for future regret. Down the line, he or she would have likely asked, "What if I had tried?" Whether you realize it or not, you have the power right now to avoid this kind of regret. That power rests largely on your ability to set and execute goals! So, the question is, how can you do this effectively?

When setting goals, it is important that you are as honest with yourself as possible. Let's consider our three factors for setting good goals: (1) vision, (2) belief, and (3) commitment. In general, your belief and commitment act as a system of "checks and balances" for your vision. If you don't believe that you can accomplish something, then you will not act on it. Furthermore, if you assess that you don't have the talent, then you cannot truly believe that you can accomplish the goal. Likewise, if you are not willing to develop the necessary skills to accomplish your goal, then you are not committed.

The capacity to measure progress is a key aspect to any real goal. However, this can be convoluted. On one hand, progress is akin to developing skills and cultivating talents that are required to meet a goal; on the other hand, individuals can achieve goals by means other than their own talents and skills. While this can produce great results, this can also be counterproductive. Why do I say this? Because reliance on someone else for the talent and skills that are directly associated with making progress on your goals robs you of the capacity to control your rate of progress. While there are instances in which this might be necessary—such as paying someone to do work that saves you time—ensuring that you can control the rate of progress on your goals will help you stay focused on the right goals.

The principle of controlling your rate of progress is integral to your success. By grasping it, you will begin to see the world—and your own personal responsibility for learning—differently. The following is an example of a circumstance in my life in which I was not able to control the rate of progress and was devastated by it. Towards the end of my almost 8-year stint in the engineering field I decided that I wanted to be the CEO of a technology company. I had been developing an idea for a mobile app within the span of that last year and I thought I was ready to work on it full-time. The only problem was that I had very little experience with computer programming, or "coding," which was the main skill I needed to make progress. I learned how to do all the other stuff—develop a business plan, establish an LLC, build a website, etc.—but I did not have the main ingredient! Consequently, I ended up using most of the financial savings I had accrued over my 8 years of work to pay someone else to build the app. Furthermore, because I was not building it myself, I had no control over the timeframe in which it was built. It ended up being an extreme strain on my time, energy, and money, and I eventually had to put it on the back burner while I rebuilt the professional life I had destroyed in pursuit of that endeavor.

So, what exactly happened? At first glance, my pursuit of the mobile app company probably seems harmless. My goal of building the company seemed to align with the vision I had for my life to make a positive impact on communities and students, and I believed that I could build a successful company. However, looking back, the fact that I didn't have the basic skillset that would enable me to control the rate of progress for my company should have been a red flag. And the reality was that I wasn't truly committed enough to develop the necessary skills. If I was committed, I would have been willing to learn the rudiments of computer programming to build the app, no matter how long it took me. Instead, I chose to allow my rate of progress to be determined by someone else.

I cannot emphasize enough the importance of regulating progress. In the case of my failed mobile app idea, I was "playing a waiting game." I could call meetings, I could share ideas for making modifications to the app, and I could even offer incentives for faster development, but, at the end of the day, I had very little control over the development of the app. Therefore, I was not in control of the company that I sought to build.

Time Management

Assessing your progress is an integral aspect of goal setting. Once you have established a goal in which you can regulate progress with your talents and skills, it is important that you gauge that progress. While you may not initially have an idea of how long it will take you to accomplish a goal, you can establish a process that will help you measure the rate at which you are making progress. To do this, you must set boundaries for working towards your goal. Earlier we defined boundaries as the "rules you set for yourself to ensure you continue to make progress." In terms of goal setting, these boundaries are the time constraints you must establish for working on your goals. This is especially important when you have goals that don't have a set deadline. For instance, when I started writing my first book, I didn't know how long it would take me. However, I gave myself two hours a day to write, and, once I got into a rhythm, I was able to gauge how much I could accomplish over a certain time span (i.e., weeks, months, etc.)

Frankly, to execute your goals you must have a sense of urgency, or desperation—not in the sense of being anxious, but in the sense of not putting off what you know needs to be done. Highly successful people live life like this. They have an undeniable vigor to succeed at what they do. This is not always communicated outwardly in unbridled passion, but many times it is conveyed through quiet diligence in the work at hand. Nonetheless, this unwillingness to be denied their goals allows them to endure the hardships of the process. This must be your mentality! That is why it is extremely important for your goals to be based on your vision. Furthermore, as we discussed earlier in the book, you must believe you can achieve whatever you are going after. Regarding goal setting, a lack of belief will result in either not setting goals or not following through with them. In the case of my first book, I finally had a goal that was based on something I believed in—I not only had a desire, but I envisioned myself writing it, and I had an unyielding belief that it was meant for me to write it. This sense of purpose invigorated me to stick to the time constraints I had defined for myself.

How well you execute your goals has everything to do with how well you plan the use of your time and follow through with it. This is where discipline comes in. When I wrote my first book, I always wrote for two hours at a time because I recognized that this was what I needed to ensure that I gave myself enough time to connect my thoughts. That time commitment wasn't always convenient, but even when I didn't feel like writing I knew I had to sit down and write. Oftentimes I would start at 7 a.m., but sometimes it was 5 a.m., and sometimes even 3 a.m. While I took a break for days at a time, and sometimes even a week or two, my mindset never changed—I stayed in the process.

Planning

Your goals can have as many or as few steps as needed to make them feasible for you. In the case of our earlier example of the aspiring singer, he or she may have determined a goal of winning a singing contest. Naturally, he or she would have needed to set some boundaries for preparing for each contest. Much like me writing my first book, he or she would have needed to operate within those boundaries to measure progress. That is, each performance would indicate how much, if any, he or she needed to increase time spent rehearsing.

Ironically, the difference between achieving goals and not achieving them is often a matter of taking incremental steps. Many people don't achieve goals because they get so hung up on "how to get started" that they never actually start. The key is that each step should be simple enough for you to act in lieu of feeling so overwhelmed that you don't do anything. Generally, your progress should be monitored by setting benchmarks. A benchmark can be defined as "a specific deadline or a time constraint for taking specific actions." For instance, in our example of the aspiring singer, the benchmark set might have been for him or her to compete in at least one contest per month.

To move forward more efficiently, you may need to do some research before you start. This may help you gain clarity and momentum. For example, many individuals with business ideas don't know where to start. As a result, those ideas just stay in their heads and never manifest. However, with just a little research, those individuals might be able to simplify their goal into steps that enable them to act. The following is an example of how a goal might be organized by steps for someone wanting to become a blogger, a person that frequently publishes written content online with a particular scope or topic.

Objective: Become a blogger		
Goal: Start blog		
Steps	**Benchmark/Deadline**	**Boundaries**
Research how to blog	1 week from present day	30 minutes per day (M-F)
Set up blog site	3 weeks from present day	30 minutes per day (M-F)
Make first blog post	1 month from present day	30 minutes per day (M-F)

The benchmark in this example represents the amount of time this individual might give themselves to accomplish a certain step within his or her goal of becoming a blogger. Notice that the last column depicts the boundaries that one might set. From our example, we see that once this individual accomplishes the step of researching how to blog he or she can then move to the next step of setting up a blog site. Furthermore, after he or she makes the first post, the number of posts made per week can be regulated by modifying the boundaries. For instance, he or she may determine a need to write for an hour per day in lieu of 30 minutes per day to increase the number of posts per week.

Whether you realize it or not, you have what you need to start setting and achieving some goals right now. All you need is a little self-reflection. Chances are that you, as well as your friends, teachers and family, can all see patterns in your life that indicate your real interests and talents. Now, you simply must take the time to identify those patterns and start setting some goals to move in that direction.

SELF-REFLECTION

14. What are your interests (e.g., things you feel passionate about, either regarding a career or how you want to make an impact in the world)?

15. What are some of your talents and skills? Do you have any evidence of this? Explain.

16. How do your talents and skills support your interests?

17. Based on the above, what careers can you imagine yourself possibly having? What would your duties entail? Be as creative and detailed as possible.

CHAPTER 5—RELATING SCHOOL WITH GOALS

Compliance

Earlier we discussed the purpose of school. Hopefully, since then you

have begun evaluating why it is important to you. Now we will dig a little

deeper in discussing how your personal goals are directly connected to

what you do in school. First off, do you know the sole purpose of

teachers, principals, and counselors? They are in place to help prepare

you for life. While it may often feel like school staff don't care about your

opinion, more times than not they want to understand your perspective of

school so that they can better help you achieve your goals.

Since you are developing the "big picture" for what you want out of life, it

is now time to identify the resources that can help you. Whether you

agree with how your principal runs your school or not, the reality of the

purpose of school is simple—it is there to provide you with subject matter

that will broaden your perspective of the world and develop basic skills

needed for success in life. Now, here's the catch: You have a large part to

play in how effective school is for you.

Contrary to what it may seem, you are entitled to feel however you want to feel about school. However, if your perspective is negatively affecting your overall performance then it is counterproductive to your personal development and well-being. Therefore, it is important to develop a healthy perspective of school and how it relates to your life. Consider the following questions: Have you ever wondered why you like some classes more than others? Could it be that those classes relate to something you are really interested in? Now is the time to find the correlations between your interests and the courses (and extracurricular activities) that will provide you with the knowledge and skills development to move in the direction of your vision. As you do this you can begin setting some goals for self-improvement in those areas.

Responsibility

Believe it or not, your courses are directly related to what you want to do in life. Naturally, since you are just getting a feel for what you want out of life, you may not quite know where to start in determining the correlation between your interests and the classroom. That's exactly why school is right where you need to be! In fact, helping you make this connection is the expertise of your guidance counselors. In addition, your teachers may be able to provide some helpful insight through classroom instruction. You should try asking your teachers to explain certain concepts in a way that relates more to the real world. If your questions are specific enough, they will likely take you up on that challenge. As you begin to broaden your perspective of the world around you through utilizing your resources—at school and at home—you will become more effective in setting goals that align with the direction you want to go in life.

Earlier we discussed the importance of school and the opportunity you have to receive a formal education. Considering this, you have an opportunity to build the educational experience you want! Let me explain. Have you ever thought of what your school day might look like if you could design it? What would you choose to learn about? Now that you have an idea of what you want, maybe you are starting to see the benefits of hours of classroom instruction. On the other hand, maybe you see a need for a totally different approach. Bottom line, you are now more equipped to think critically about how school can help you achieve the vision for your life. While parents, teachers, and principles are there to help you, you hold the keys to placing value on your learning experience.

The following is an example of setting personal goals that can be enhanced and supported through school. For a moment, let's assume that you have an interest in being a psychologist, someone who studies how the brain works to help individuals work through challenging thoughts, feelings, and behaviors. Now let's say that you are a struggling math student, but after doing your research on this occupation you realize that it requires advanced analytical skills that typically are indicative of those who perform well in math. Naturally upon this discovery you may conclude that you need to set a goal to start doing more math activities. But what if you don't like math because it doesn't make sense to you? Do you then totally abandon your interest in psychology? Well, that depends on how serious you are about pursuing it! If you are serious, then this would be the time to get help in math—school is one of the few places in which help can be made available if you ask. On the other hand, if you are not serious then this would be the time to reevaluate your interests.

In the previous scenario, learning that psychology required math played an integral role in bringing about a point of decision. If math was a deterrent, then that may have revealed a lack of commitment to pursuing psychology. Making this inference would have helped you save time and energy that you could have used towards another career interest. It only takes a little understanding about your interests to start you on the path of setting the right career goals. In the same way, your ability to take full advantage of your academic opportunities begins with an honest assessment of how school relates to your interests. In seeking the answer to this, you will discover your strengths, weaknesses, and opportunities for growth both personally and academically.

SELF-REFLECTION

18. Identify some resources at school that are available to you right now for learning and self-improvement. List them below. (These resources can be specific people, places, or things.)

19. What skills do you think you need to develop that are related to your goals?

20. What classes do you think are most helpful in building those skills?

21. What would you like to learn most in those classes?

TOPIC 2: WHO'S COMING WITH YOU?

CHAPTER 6—IDENTIFYING POSITIVE AND NEGATIVE INFLUENCES

Prudence

You may have heard the adage, "Birds of a feather flock together." I cannot stress enough how true this is. Looking back at my life, I can clearly see how my habits have conformed to those whom I have been around on a continuous basis. This phenomenon has been consistent even at times when I have recognized the habit and have made a conscious decision not to pick it up. Looking back, I see how people that were lazy rubbed that laziness off on me. I also see how people that were optimistic passed that optimism to me. Whether you realize it or not, you can be affected by those you are around even if you are not engaging in direct communication with them! Earlier we briefly looked at some hypothetical examples of what might happen to an individual under different influences, negative and positive. Now we will look at how to identify these influences even when they are not very clear.

"Birds of a feather flock together."

If you want to make the most of your current opportunities, then it is important that you understand how your influences drastically affect the decisions you make, whether positive or negative. Now that you have determined what you want, the question you must ask yourself is, "Who is coming with me?" In answering this question, it is integrally important to be able to identify your positive and negative influences. It is also important for you to know that at times even mature, well-accomplished adults struggle with differentiating positive and negative influences. With all the hustle and bustle of life, it is easy for information to become cluttered in the mind leaving individuals torn between who to listen to. Nonetheless, the better you do this now the more effective you will be in positioning yourself to be successful in achieving what you want. So, here is the basis of what you need to know: Positive influences help you get to where you want to go, and negative influences don't!

It would be virtually impossible to identify some of these influences without having an idea of the direction you want to go. In the case of negative influences, many of them might seem like they are the right people or places to be around. They may make you comfortable, and even make you feel good, but that doesn't mean they are good for you. Fortunately, we spent the first section of this book focusing on helping you establish what you want out of life, as well as better understand how to use school to launch you towards it. Now that you have this foundation, you are equipped to begin identifying the difference between negative and positive influences.

Foremost, those with the potential to be negative influences for your life are individuals or groups whose habits are not in line with the practices you have identified as key to helping you accomplish your goals—these individuals simply don't share a similar vision with you for their lives. Therefore, how you spend your time should look much different than how they spend their time. When considering separating yourself from negative influences it is important to understand that this is not a matter of neglecting people. Rather, it is a matter of acknowledging ways that you cannot open yourself up to those people. You can still support and care for them without being negatively influenced by them. Giving yourself a little breathing room from them may seem difficult at first but, as you experience some success with your goals and better understand the practices required to get to where you want to go, the need for this will become clearer.

In the case that you have family members that are negative influences, you may not be able to just eliminate your exposure to them. For instance, you may live in the same house with someone that demeans you with their words. While you may not be able to reduce your exposure, you can develop the strength to resist believing some of the negative things they may say. By recognizing that those words are not in line with what you want out of life and what you are striving to believe, you have the power to minimize their effects. As you practice combatting this negativity, you will empower yourself through your own beliefs and words.

Humility

Now, let's discuss positive influences. I will begin with an analogy. Imagine that you were the laughingstock of the school. All day you encountered students laughing at you as you walked by, and you didn't know why. Finally, a close friend approached you and told you the reason why people had been laughing. How do you think you would feel towards your friend at that moment? Would you get mad at your friend because he or she brought it to your attention? Or would your initial response be one of gratitude, since they cared enough to tell you? While you may know deep down inside that your friend delivered the message out of sincerity, you might initially feel negatively towards them because of how you feel in the moment. We all have had times in our lives in which we have taken offense to what somebody has said to us and, yet, when we really thought about it we realized that the person had made a valid point.

So, why were we offended? In many cases, that offense comes because that person is challenging what we believe about ourselves. Contrary to how it may feel, this is actually a good thing. Having this mental exchange is necessary for growth in life. We need people in our lives who will challenge our way of thinking, even though it is often painful. You may have heard the saying, "The truth hurts." Well, many times it does!

"The truth hurts."

If you have people that "keep it real"—and you know it comes from a place of honesty and not ridicule—then these are your real friends. Identify them and keep them around. You don't necessarily have to spend a lot of time with them, but these are the people you will want to talk to about your interests and goals. Their constructive criticism will help you perfect your roadmap to success, if you allow it to.

If you have known someone for years, it can be tough to evaluate the magnitude of their influence on you. Nonetheless, their influence may have even affected your thought patterns over time. In evaluating this influence, you may need to think back some years and look at who and what has influenced some of the decisions you have made. You may find that you don't like the results. As you begin making choices for your betterment, you will gain the strength to break free from negative influences (and its consequences) and begin embracing those positive influences that so often are neglected. Once you start manifesting positive results from your decisions, you may even be able to help those that once had a negative influence on you.

SELF-REFLECTION

22. Do you have people in your life that build your self-esteem, encourage you to make good decisions, and support you even when you make a mistake? What are their main characteristics?

23. Do you have people in your life that tear you down? What are their characteristics?

24. Considering the above, what are the main differences between those that support you and those that tear you down?

CHAPTER 7—PEER PRESSURE

Responsibility

There are countless stories of crimes committed by individuals who didn't want to do them but were influenced by their "so-called" friends. The sad part is that many times those individuals must still suffer the consequences of their actions. Maybe you have heard of cases like this. Maybe you have even been involved in one. Peer pressure is a powerful form of negative influence that can cause individuals to do things that they know are wrong and that they really don't want to do.

Many students are vulnerable to peer pressure because of the myriads of challenges that school and family life pose. For instance, even if you aren't challenged academically, you probably have at least experienced insecurities about social acceptance or distress from circumstance at home. Sadly, students all over the world make drastic decisions due to this reality. Knowing that under the right amount of pressure you have the capacity to do something out of character, it is important that you consider how you are influenced by peer pressure both in and out of school. Furthermore, while your actions may be a product of peer pressure, avoiding its unwanted consequences is still your responsibility.

Self-awareness

It can be hard to admit that you are being influenced by peer pressure. Most students probably would like to think that they are in full control and don't care that much about what others think. Well, that is just not reality. You care! Most students care. If you're honest with yourself, you can admit that you have allowed others to depict your actions in some way. We all have! Once you acknowledge this then you can begin figuring out how to regain control of your decisions and actions. To start identifying peer pressure you may need to evaluate how your peers are affecting your ability to reach your goals. For instance, if you know you should be making all A's, but you are making C's or D's because you're hanging out with students that don't have the same goals then you need to consider making some changes.

You may even need some assistance in removing yourself from the control of peer pressure. You may have questions like, "How do I separate myself after all this time?" or "How do I tell that person that I need some space?" These are great questions to have. Your guidance counselors are there to help you break free from the burdens of peer pressure. As they understand the levels of peer pressure that you and your peers deal with, they can better work with teachers and administrators to create a better learning environment. Furthermore, this is not the time to be worried about what your peers think about you. When it is all said and done, your real friends will be there to support you. Make the necessary changes now. This is for your life and your future.

SELF-REFLECTION

25. Have you ever been peer pressured at school to do something you did not want to do?

26. How often are you peer pressured at school?

27. Can you identify some ways that you are peer pressured at school and other places? Explain.

28. Have you ever done something that you didn't want to do because of peer pressure? How did you feel afterwards? How did you cope with your feelings?

29. On a scale of 1 - 5 (5 being the most extreme) how much does peer pressure still affect you? Why do you think this is?

30. Do you want to stop allowing yourself to be peer pressured?

31. What can you do to avoid peer pressure?

32. Do you feel that you need to seek help? If so, who do you think can help?

CHAPTER 8—RESPONSIBILITY & ESTEEM

Discipline

For a moment, stop and consider all the things that you feel responsible for. Is it your family? Your grades? Your behavior? To truly understand responsibility, you must develop a healthy perspective of the things that are required of you right now. Frankly, there are some things that you are just expected to do and there is no good excuse for why you can't do them. For instance, at home it may be chores, and at school it may be homework. Every opportunity in life has its own set of requirements, some more obvious than others. In terms of manifesting the vision for your life, you must meet the requirements of each step along the way. This doesn't mean you won't fall short sometimes but understand that there are consequences for your shortcomings that affect you and those you love.

I want us to look just a little deeper into identifying responsibilities. I am going to use a metaphor to help us do that. When I was younger I was a huge basketball fan. I remember watching high school basketball players and often noticing that the players I thought were the most talented and fun to watch were not the ones that I saw go to the big colleges or play professional basketball. As I got older, I began realizing the difference between those players and the ones that became professionals. As I compared attributes, I could see a stark difference. While talent was an integral factor, it was not the defining factor. Many of the players that I watched "jump out of the gym" in high school couldn't hit an open jump shot when the game was on the line. The athleticism that had separated them in high school was overshadowed by what they could not do at the next level. There was a certain level of proficiency in fundamentals required that they had not developed. There was more that was required at the next level and, therefore, their responsibility was greater.

Now let's take school for example. Since you are in school, we will assume that you have a goal of graduating. Maybe you want this for yourself, your family, or both. Foremost, whether you like school or not, it goes without saying that you are required to achieve passing grades in order to continue making progress toward graduation. Furthermore, to pass your classes you must exemplify some level of effort to attend class and complete tasks. Along with this, you must meet the behavioral expectations of your teachers and administrators. If you don't comply with these standards, you will not be successful in your academic endeavors. Therefore, your responsibility is just as much to your compliance with behavior as it is to academics.

Regarding this example, many students have a tough time making the correlation between behavior and academics. They feel that if they do their work then they should be able to act the way they want to. Yet, the reality is that without proper behavior you can lose the privilege of doing your work. We see a similar disconnect between behavior and expectations quite frequently in the case of college athletes that have the promise of a full scholarship and then lose it all over a bad decision. While many of these scholarships even cover injury, they don't cover certain behaviors and actions that disqualify them from representing the school athletics program. Sadly, many athletes don't get the memo until it is too late.

Hopefully you are beginning to see how important it is that your perspective of responsibility aligns with what is required of you through each stage of your life. Just as conduct in class is a requirement to continue to learn in a classroom setting, society has certain requirements that you are responsible to meet to maintain your privileges as a citizen and a contributing member of society. These are the laws that are in place and the unwritten rules that govern social behavior. I have noticed in schools that many students already express their disdain for following these standards. While it is okay to not agree with some things, you need to always try to understand why you don't agree. Not abiding by what is required will always have consequences, whether legal or social. Therefore, if you are going to suffer those consequences then it needs to be for a cause that you truly value.

Compliance

When the rules are not abusive or hurtful, you must learn to abide by them and use them to your advantage and not your demise. Unlike laws that are challenged in society for ethical reasons, the rules that you deal with at school are generally for the betterment of you and your peers. It is your responsibility to abide by them so that you can continue to benefit from the opportunity of a formal education. Ironically, many times I have heard students complain about why they must walk in a single file line in the hallway or sit in assigned seats. "We aren't kids," they rant! Whether you realize it or not, your teachers and administrators are forced to put rules in place because most students cannot handle the freedom that they desire. For instance, many teachers assign seats in the classroom because, without this constraint, they know that their students would cause more interruptions than are tolerable. Moreover, in many circumstances, school and classroom rules such as "no talking in the hallway" or "no getting up out of your seat without permission" are necessary to maintain order.

While you may feel that these rules infringe on your freedom, they are there to provide a safe and healthy learning environment for you and your peers. There is an old saying that suggests individuals adopt the rules and procedures of wherever they are to preserve their well-being: "When in Rome, do as the Romans do." Well, school is Rome! You must learn to accept the rules. If you don't then you will reap the consequences. Moreover, if you want to graduate and be prepared for the next step in your life, then it is a responsibility to yourself and to your family to abide by those rules.

If you are struggling to abide by rules now, it is not going to get any easier out there in society. I have seen students continually break rules and then get mad when there are consequences. Yet, if being honest, those same students would admit that they know their behavior is counterproductive for themselves, a distraction to other students, and is deserving of the consequences. Bottom line, while students may criticize many of the rules that are set in place, these rules address "negative" behaviors that students tend to struggle to control. Therefore, knowing this, students must begin

"When in Rome, do as the Romans do."

to take responsibility for their actions in lieu of challenging those in authority. If many students would simply accept the rules of the classroom—instead of resisting them—they might discover that the world is not against them, even though it often feels that way.

Diligence

So far throughout this book you have been challenged to form goals that you feel good about working towards. In doing so, hopefully you have begun to accept that it is your responsibility to avoid the things that you know will hinder you from achieving your goals. However, if you do not keep in mind why you have those goals then you can easily become irresponsible with the opportunities you have been afforded. Earlier in the book we defined vision as "knowing what you want out of life." Well, regarding being responsible with opportunities, it is important that you hold fast to your vision so that you can be motivated to keep being responsible. Furthermore, if you don't do this you can easily fall into the trap of making excuses for why you don't maximize opportunities, and, more times than not, your challenges will become reasons to quit.

The stronger your vision is the better you will define your responsibilities. To better clarify the role that vision plays, let's examine some typical challenges that individuals face on their jobs. You may find this strikingly like your experiences at school. Overbearing bosses (teachers), coworkers (students) that may be hard to get along with, and unfavorable hours (classes) are all aspects that working class adults deal with at some point in their professional lives. If individuals don't have a solid objective (i.e., an expected outcome), when times get hard it can seem easy for them to leave a job that is their best opportunity at that moment. On the contrary, if they are moving towards their vision and, thereby, have defined a solid objective for that job—such as to generate income for their family or improve skills that will help them get the next job—they will be better motivated to endure amidst challenges and continue upholding responsibilities. In the same way, your vision is integral to you maximizing your potential at school.

By this point in your life hopefully you have begun to realize that you are not just living for yourself. While you must help yourself first, your existence is for the bigger picture—you are living for your family and the legacy you will leave behind for your children and those that will follow in your footsteps. Just as you have individuals who you admire, there are some individuals that look up to you. Therefore, your responsibility is also to them. When considering your decisions, you should consider how those that depend on you for support, encouragement, and guidance are affected by those decisions. This should factor into the decisions you make and should serve as a driving force in you taking the necessary actions to be responsible with the opportunities you have been afforded. Now that you are aware of how school can be used to help you, there is no excuse for not using it to attain what you want out of life. You alone are in control of your actions and there is no more valuable time than now to make sure you are taking the right ones.

SELF-REFLECTION

33. What things are you responsible for right now in your life?

34. Are there people that look up to you as a leader or role model? Make a list. What are their expectations of you?

35. What have you identified as the responsibilities you have to yourself? Explain.

36. On a scale of 1-5 (with 5 being the best), how do you feel about yourself overall?

37. Explain in a few short sentences why you feel this way about yourself.

38. Do you think your feelings about yourself help or hurt you? Explain.

39. What things could possibly help build your self-esteem? Explain.

40. Would you like help in these areas?

CHAPTER 9—APPRECIATING YOUR SUPPORTERS

Gratitude

In previous chapters we discussed how you might identify the individuals that you need to spend your time with based on a common vision and goals. Now we will identify the people that have supported you thus far. In a society driven by self-gratification, those that extend moral support are often overlooked. Many individuals even struggle to decipher the line between celebrating their own efforts and acknowledging those that helped them along the way. Nonetheless, it is important that you express your appreciation to the individuals that have helped you and reciprocate the love and support they have shown.

Sadly, many times the quiet service of individuals goes unnoticed amidst the clamor of all the other people in our lives sucking our time and energy. Whether you feel like it or not, you didn't get here by yourself! Your journey here may not have been pretty, and you may not have received the accolades that you felt you deserved, but you have had help; else, you would not still be alive. If you think hard enough, you will begin to see those I am talking about. Your real supporters are the ones that have tried to guide you down the right path, whether through constructive criticism or unyielding support. These individuals may not share the characteristics of the crowd that you typically hang around—and they may not have always agreed with what you have said and done—but they have always been there.

Humility

Regarding your progression in personal success, part of being responsible is nurturing your positive relationships. You never know when you will need these individuals. The first step to this is acknowledgment. Many people have a hard time admitting they need help or even asking for it. I admit to this myself. For a long time in my life, my self-sufficient attitude and stubbornness did not allow me to even recognize that I needed help. Consequently, I am sure I "reinvented the wheel" thousands of times in my life when there was already an available solution that would have made things a lot easier. One memory of this stands out to me because of the ramifications I can now identify throughout my life. I was in 8th grade and my mom came up to my school for a quarterly parent-teacher meeting for my Algebra class. I was an "A" student (borderline) so I was doing fine, but my binder was a mess! My teacher brought that to my mom's attention and showed us the binder of the top student—his grade in the class was a 99. His binder was impeccable, totally the opposite of mine. My teacher keyed in on how, if I would adopt that type of organization, I would improve my grade in the class. While that was nice to know, I was not really interested in help from anyone—I was doing it my way, and I was fine!

Knowing what I know now about life, I should have taken the time to talk with that student about his binder and learn how I might apply some of his methods to improve mine. I am almost sure that I have since had to learn those organizational skills the hard way many times over. Nonetheless, I am glad to say that I am much better now at learning from others, and I hope it does not take you as long as it did me. By developing an instinct to ask for help when I am unsure of how to do something well, I save a tremendous amount of time and energy.

As I have learned to work with others, I have also realized that it is more beneficial to reap the benefits of teamwork than to prove what I can do on my own. Ironically, I credit this resolution to my introduction to the education profession. My first stint at teaching forced me into desperation—I needed help. After much resistance, I finally succumbed to seeking out materials that had already been developed. Since then, I no longer need to feel desperate before I ask for help. Furthermore, I now embrace the concept of having a support system that can help me with both work and home life. In the same way, your supporters are there for you to learn from and lean on. It is a splendid thing to be able to learn from someone else's mistakes, so you do not have to repeat them. I encourage you to adopt this mentality of building a support system now by taking inventory of your needs and those around you who can be of assistance.

Now that we have dealt with the issue of acknowledging the need for help and support, we will focus on how you can show your supporters that you care. Frankly, sometimes it can be hard to do this. Some of your supporters may not be as open to receiving help in the ways that you can offer it. That's okay. Furthermore, it takes planning to show appreciation. I have always struggled with this! For instance, sometimes I want to call family members to check on them—and even write it down on my agenda—but still will not do it! Frankly, the necessary things are typically not convenient. Time must be made for them, and it takes a continued effort. Yet, that effort is minuscule compared to the benefits. As you get older, growing responsibilities and less disposable time will make it even harder to build meaningful relationships. By building these relationships now, you can get an early start on what takes some people decades to realize the importance of.

To frame all of this, I want to share a brief story. Some years after I finished college, I rented out a house with a few other guys. Well, one of them was going through some relationship troubles. Not really thinking too much of it, I gave him some encouraging advice and let him know that I was there for him if he needed anything. I did not know it at the time, but my words really impacted him in a way that helped him overcome some significant hurdles. While we were merely acquaintances at the time, years later he is now a close friend of mine. My encouragement to him had served as a foundation for a strong bond, and he has since reciprocated that by showing his appreciation over the years. Ironically, just a few years after I helped him, he was able to help me through a tough time.

While many people try to win friendship and respect through their authority or popularity, showing appreciation will win you loyal friends that will be there when it matters. Later in life you will want the people who have supported you to remain in your corner. You will also want them to have a desire to have you in their corner. You never know how meaningful a gesture of your appreciation may be to someone who has helped you. It may change their life to know that you noticed what they did and that you cared enough to say something. Therefore, I encourage you right now to take the time to consider those who have supported you and show your appreciation. A simple card or phone call is oftentimes more than enough. While showing your appreciation only takes a moment

it can yield results that last a lifetime.

SELF-REFLECTION

41. Take a moment and consider those who have encouraged and supported you over the years (e.g., family, peers, mentors, etc.). Make a list of these individuals.

42. Do you feel that you have shown your appreciation to them enough? Why?

43. Do you set time aside to spend with those who support you the most? If so, how much?

44. Do you exemplify the same support to them that they do to you? If so, how? If not, what can you do to improve this?

45. Briefly describe what you can do to make showing appreciation and support for others a regular practice in your life.

CHAPTER 10—COMMUNITY

Perspective

Where are you from? This is a source of pride for most individuals.

There is something special about where we are raised. No matter what our

circumstances are at home, there is a special place in our hearts for the

people and surroundings that form our perspective of the world. I posed

that first question because the answer to it is critical to understanding the

challenges you face and the opportunities you have for growth and

development. There is a saying you may be familiar with, "If you don't

know your past then you are bound to repeat it." In the same way, if you

don't know the common pitfalls of your community then you are at risk of

falling right into them. The reality is that your community is typically

what shapes you. That is, what you see, hear, and feel every day is how

you are inclined to perceive the world.

Your community encompasses the environments you are accustomed to

experiencing every day such as your home, neighborhood, and school. In

fact, often the culture of a school takes on the character of its

"If you don't know your past then you are bound to repeat it."

surroundings. In neighborhoods that are riddled with high jobless rates and crime—where students are more concerned with the safety and well-being of their families than they are with academic success—students may be less focused in the classroom. On the other hand, in middle and upper-class neighborhoods—where students have less of these concerns—there is a greater capacity for them to be more focused on the daily demands of the classroom. In this regard, the battle for your future has more to do with your ability to develop a sober perspective of your community than it does your experiences in the classroom. In fact, up until this point in your life, this perspective has likely determined how you view the classroom.

So, what does this mean for you? Well, right now you have a choice to open your eyes and see your community for what it is and decide if you are going to be a product of it or not. Does your community look like what you want your life to be? Do the places you go to and the people you see reflect what you want for you and your family? Earlier we discussed how our response to influences, both positive and negative, can form our belief over time. Unfortunately, many students fall victim to beliefs that are consistent with the "negative" aspects of their environment. They start believing that school is not for them, that they will never get a fair chance, and that their only way out of tough situations is by illegal means. This belief stops them from aspiring to do well in school and eventually leads them—even if they graduate—into a life in which they are not a responsible and contributing member of society. On the contrary, you have the power to embrace the positive and avoid the negative as much as possible. In fact, you have the power to have a positive impact on your community.

Determination

Practically speaking, you should have some type of feeling toward the community in which you were raised, both good and bad. For instance, you may despise that you do not feel safe, but you may love how people in your community rally together. Your ability to acknowledge how you feel about your community has the potential to be a driving force in your motivation in and out of school. How? Well, whether your community represents the life you want or the life you do not want, this can help bring clarity to the vision you are forming for your life. Furthermore, considering these positive and negative aspects may help you discover something you are passionate about. For instance, I grew up in Birmingham, Alabama, in a low-income to lower middle-income community. One thing that always stood out to me as I rode through my neighborhood as a child was all the blight. I hated seeing dilapidated buildings and boarded-up storefronts. It was depressing. This ignited a passion in me early on to be a catalyst for change in my community and other communities that looked like it.

Can you identify something in your community that you would like to change? How would that improve the living situations of people? Consider what you feel helps or hinders the quality of life for you and others in your community as well as what you can do to make a positive contribution. In addition, by helping to develop a solution to a problem you can help yourself avoid making decisions that perpetuate the problem.

You have the power to begin changing your community through your ideas. As you choose to expose yourself to positive influences, you will begin to generate ideas that reflect those influences and will affect others in a positive way. Moreover, school can then become an incubator for your ideas. This may encompass a combination of reaching out to teachers, principals, and counselors, as well as collaborating with other students. Working alongside your peers can be a driving force for the success of everyone involved. As you do this, you will begin to understand how progressing towards a shared vision helps everyone bring their skills to the table and make progress on their individual goals.

The same character traits that are required for you to be able to set goals and execute them in the classroom are the same ones that you will need to bring about changes in your community. Therefore, your hard work in school will translate to your ability to help your community. There are opportunities awaiting you to step in and contribute. All you need now is to determine a change that you are motivated to see happen!

Earlier I mentioned that there are individuals who admire you and look up to you. For a moment, consider who those individuals are. Is it a younger sibling? Is it a cousin? Is it a friend that you know is going down the wrong path? Remember, they are listening and watching. They are the members of your community that need you the most right now. As you consider your well-being, consider theirs. How can you set an example for them to follow? You have the power to help them establish a path to success as you firmly establish yours.

SELF-REFLECTION

46. Do you believe you are responsible for taking care of your community?

47. How do you feel about your community? Why?

48. Do you believe your community has helped you? How?

49. Do you believe your community has hindered you? How?

50. How do you think social media has had a positive or negative effect on your community? Explain.

51. Have you noticed how actions of certain individuals have affected your community in a positive or negative way? If so, name some of the actions and outcomes.

52. What ideas do you have for how you can make a positive impact?

53. Why do you want to make that impact?

54. Can you envision your actions affecting your community in the long run? Describe what that might look like.

TOPIC 3: WHAT WILL YOU DO?

CHAPTER 11—TIME MANAGEMENT

Persistence

Now that you have built some perspective, it is time to apply strategies to put your newfound knowledge into practice. You know what to do, but the question is, "What will you do?" Only you can decide that. What will your commitment to reading this book amount to, when it is all said and done? The answer to this question revolves around how you choose to use your time from now on. If you really think about it, everything we have gone over so far has dealt with forming a perspective that will affect how you use your time. Time governs everything we do and is, therefore, the most important commodity we will ever have. We cannot get it back! While more money can be made, time keeps ticking away. Therefore, we must be intentional with how we use it if we want to be successful in our endeavors.

By this point in your life, you have heard the term "time management." Whether you know it or not, you use time management every day. In some regard, you manage your time to prep for school each day, to participate in extracurricular activities, and to complete tasks such as household chores and homework. Nonetheless, regarding the pursuit of the life you want, there is so much more to be understood about how time management affects your progress. We will start with this example: We all know that professional athletes work hard to train. The question is, "Why?" Well, if we consider how small their critical years of development are—from about 7 to 18 years old—they don't have much room for error. That is, they do not have time to waste! They must keep pushing to get better and learn from their failures and shortcomings. If they are going to make it, then they cannot afford to take a year off because of discouragement or fear. They must stay focused. Typically, those that are successful have strong coaches, parents, and mentors holding them accountable for how they use their time.

Even if you do not aspire to be a professional athlete, you should adopt a similar mindset for your time. Contrary to what it may seem right now, everything you want out of life is time sensitive. In fact, opportunities you are not even aware of can be passing you by right now. If you want to take advantage of as many opportunities as possible to build the life you want, then you will have to master the art of managing your time. Otherwise, you will be forced to settle for less.

Goal-setting

We have discussed vision and goals throughout this book. In mastering time management, it is integral that your vision and goals are time oriented. That is, you should set goals that help you achieve what you want in the amount of time you want it. For instance, you may have 1-year, 3-year, or even weekly and monthly goals. Furthermore, as you begin envisioning what you want your life to look like at certain points in time, or "benchmarks," you can then begin strategically setting goals that are consistent with producing that outcome. While there is no guarantee that things will go as projected, setting these boundaries will help you measure your progress and endure the process of pursuing what you want.

To better understand the importance of setting time-oriented goals, consider a car racing video game. Can you remember the first time you ever played one? You probably ran into the wall a time or two and you did not finish anywhere close to the top. Whether you have played or not, here is what I want you to think about: race car games typically have what are referred to as "checkpoints." As players go around the track, they are given a time limit for reaching each checkpoint. If a player does not reach a checkpoint in time they are eliminated from competition. Just as checkpoints help measure progress on the track, goals can help you do the same for your life.

We will now look at checkpoints in more detail to better understand the importance of setting time-oriented goals. When playing a race car game for the first time, not making it to a checkpoint in time can be a good thing. Why? Well, since your driving skills are not yet polished, early elimination can serve to reduce frustration and discouragement in the learning process. Imagine being a new player and having to endure the entire race without checkpoints. That might take forever! There would be no cars around you because they would all have already finished the race, and you would be steadily bumping into walls with no gauge of how much longer you must go. Having this as a first experience might be so discouraging that you would not even try it again.

Much like a race without checkpoints, when you do not set goals the process towards your vision can seem overwhelming and unattainable. On the other hand, when you set goals you can measure progress and develop an accurate perspective of your potential. Considering the race car game, being eliminated when you don't reach a checkpoint within the allotted time during a race can help you stay focused on sharpening your skills. With a little practice you will make that first checkpoint and then be able to move on to the next one. Eventually, you will be able to stick with the other cars and even win! In the same way, setting time-oriented goals can help you develop the skills and talents necessary for whatever you want to do in life.

Do you see the importance of these checkpoints? This is the proper use of goal setting. No matter how talented you are at something it will have to be honed through practice. Furthermore, there will always be certain skills that need to be developed alongside your talents for you to operate at a high level. This is especially relevant in your career and is a huge reason why school is relevant for you. Right now, school provides you with some obvious checkpoints. Each grade level requires mastery of certain skills. However, many students miss these checkpoints and stumble through to graduation only to get there and realize that they do not have the skills needed to function independently in society.

Another example of this disparity can be seen in the case of some professional athletes. While in recent years there has been more emphasis placed on personal development of players, in the past many of them were able to bypass the mastery of academic requirements. As a result, they didn't have the life skills needed to sustain themselves professionally and maintain a decent quality of life after retirement. Unfortunately, after years of playing a sport in which they had earned much more money than the average person, they were in dire financial straits without basic on-the-job skills and unable to support their families in a healthy way.

Time Management

Now that we have covered the importance of setting time-oriented goals,

let's discuss some obstacles. Frankly, many individuals don't set goals

because they are "waiting for a better time." Unfortunately, when

individuals do this, they typically keep putting the goal off and end up

never making progress on it. When they finally understand what is

required, many opportunities have passed them by and accomplishing

what they want is more challenging than before. On the contrary, the

reality is that there is no better time than the present! By setting small

goals that align with your vision now, you can make the process of

meeting milestones more practical and can build confidence along the

way.

It goes without saying that if you are not setting goals then you are not

participating in the race for manifesting your vision. Think about that for

a moment. Since your goals should reflect your vision, you are wasting

time if you are not meeting those goals. While some of your interests may

be consistent throughout life, time is not so kind. Individuals simply can't do the things at 60 years-old that they could at 20. Therefore, once you decide to set time-oriented goals you must also be able to manage your time well enough to fit those goals into your daily schedule and make steady progress. Therefore, if you want to make any progress at all in building the life you want it is important that you consistently evaluate your time and manage it wisely.

I want to share with you another story from my freshman year of college. My roommate told me something that year that I only began to understand years later. After seeing me come into our dorm room day-after-day and not do any homework, my roommate emphatically said: "You can pay now, or you can pay later!" At that time, I didn't understand what he meant. While I knew I wasn't doing my work, I didn't understand the concept of "paying later." After all, I felt like I was in control. I was choosing to be passive. Couldn't I just pick up the slack when I felt like it? There didn't have to be any repercussions for my actions, right?

It was not until I graduated college that I began to realize what my roommate meant. "Paying" was not necessarily something that had to be seen and felt—he was referring to how I used my time. He was warning me that I would have to "pay" for choosing to procrastinate when I knew I should have been doing my work. You see, time is something you will never get back, and how you spend it will always project your future. While an outsider may have looked at my first engineering job after college and thought that I "had it made," I was in anguish. While I had finished my degree in engineering, I had never envisioned myself having a desk job. In addition, I had not developed the work ethic that was needed to work 8 hours a day for 5 days a week! I struggled to stay on task, and I did not like seeing my supervisor coming because I knew he would be looking over my shoulder. It was agonizing. I was "paying later!" Because I had not used my time wisely by applying myself in college, I had not been able to make any definitive decisions about my future. In fact, I had been too busy playing "catch up" with my work to really take a step back and establish a vision for my life.

"You can pay now, or you can pay later."

Here is a note I want you to remember: No matter what you want to do, how you manage your time will determine your success in it. Now, the only way to start managing your time effectively is to begin valuing the importance of your time. This begins with your vision. That is, you must know what you want. I didn't significantly value my time for most of my matriculation through college because I had not defined a vision. Let me explain. You have the power to attribute value to anything you want in life. While you may not realize it, you are doing this every day by how you choose to spend your time. Why is that? Since you can't get time back, it is the most valuable thing you have. Therefore, whatever you spend your time on is what you attribute value to. Simply put, you will not value what you don't spend time on, and you will not spend time on what you don't value. Furthermore, as your vision becomes clearer, the way you use your time will resonate with greater importance.

Planning

As mentioned earlier in the book, if you truly want something and believe that you can have it, there should be a passion present that compels you to spend your time on it. Time management is simply a tool to help you facilitate the pursuit of that passion through the implementation of time-oriented goals. For instance, if you were really interested in trying out for a certain sports team, and you knew when the tryout was, you would set aside a certain amount of time per week to train. In the same way, anything you really want should become a fixture in your weekly schedule in a way that allows you to still take care of your other responsibilities. This is the basis for effective time management.

Here is a simple way to begin looking at your time. You know there's 24 hours in a day. To get a quick breakdown of your free time, you must simply subtract the amount of time (in hours) your activities consume from the number 24. So, let's start with school. Let's say you're in school 8 hours a day. Let's also assume that you get approximately 8 hours of sleep. Since $8 + 8$ is 16, and $24 - 16$ is 8, you have only eight hours to do all the things you may value such as eating, spending time with family, browsing social media, and working on your goals. So, while 8 hours may seem like a lot of time it can be quickly lost if you don't plan how you will use it. For instance, social media can absorb much of this time without you even realizing it. You can probably relate to this scenario: One moment you are sitting down to respond to a comment and then three hours later you are getting up mentally drained, hungry, and wondering where the time went!

When you can manage your time properly you have the power to control your productivity. Likewise, when you do not manage it properly you lose this power. In many cases, while you may feel that you don't have enough time to get things done, it is likely that you are just not making the best use of your time. Furthermore, the better you can account for your time the better you can value it by making sure you spend the time on the things that are most important. Focusing on this will help you eliminate unnecessary activities, including time spent with those individuals that don't share the values that underscore your success.

If you want to be successful in the things you truly want, then you will have to become a master of your time. So, the question to ask yourself right now is, "Can I be spending my time better?"

SELF-REFLECTION

55. On a scale of 1-5 (5 being the best) how good would you say you manage your time? Explain?

56. One sign of wasted time is not being able to account for how you use it. Outside of school hours, list the specific activities (e.g. watching television, football practice, dinner, etc.) you spend your time on and estimate the amount of time you spend on each.

57. How do you think your use of time is affecting your life? Explain the good and the bad.

58. In particular, how do you think your use of time is affecting your academic performance?

59. What improvements can you make right now for how you use your time?

60. Are you willing to make those improvements?

61. What actions will you take to make improvements? Be specific about how these actions will help you better manage your time. For instance, if you know you have negative influences at "Place A" then you might write: 'I will go to "Place B" where I can stay focused and get support from others that have a similar mindset.'

CHAPTER 12—ACADEMIC SUCCESS

Perseverance

I can remember back in college sometimes locking myself in a room to study and, after 4 hours, only having 15 minutes of study time done. I was constantly distracted by activities outside my window, the details of the walls, and even my own thoughts. It was frustrating to try so hard and still not get the results I wanted. However, over time I began to find a rhythm and understand the strategies that worked best for me to get the results I desired. In the same way, there will always be obstacles to your academic success. Therefore, you should go ahead and accept that the road to success is not supposed to be easy.

You have probably heard the saying, "No pain, No gain." Well, that is no less true for academics than anything else. I believe that many students don't excel academically because they have not been trained to press through mental pain. When they struggle with something classroom-related they see it as an excuse to quit. Many students feel ashamed of

"No pain, no gain."

what they don't know, and they don't want to ask for help. Others have experienced so much disappointment that they don't feel like asking for help will do any good. This kind of thinking becomes habitual and eventually leads them to believe, "School is just not for me." That's just not how it should be, and it is not the type of thinking that you should accept. You can press through and get results!

I want to use a weight-lifting analogy to further explain this concept. Let's say that you can lift a maximum of 100 pounds today and you want to be able to lift 200 pounds a year from now. If you don't lift weights from now until then, do you think you will be able to lift 200 pounds? When I have presented this scenario to students in the past, most have answered with an emphatic "No!" It is common knowledge that it takes work to build muscle. The reality is that, while you may be able to lift a little more than 100 pounds due to the natural course of your physical growth and development, you won't be able to lift 200 pounds!

Making improvements in school works much like weightlifting. Yet, many students treat school like a person expecting to be able to gain significant strength in the weight room without putting in the work. It takes intentional effort to push through tough mental exercises and build mental muscle. This is a daily practice. Let's consider reading comprehension as an example. If you were reading a passage with a lot of words that you didn't understand, then naturally it would seem hard because you would be stretching your brain beyond its current capacity. Instead of concluding that it was too hard, that would be the time to get out your dictionary and refuse to be denied! The same goes for any academic area you may struggle in. If math is not making sense that doesn't mean that math is not "your thing"—you may just need a different perspective! You may simply need to get some help. This must be your mindset if you want to excel in the classroom and develop the character needed to have continued success in school and in life.

Planning

Now that we have built some perspective of adversity in academics, let's deal with why overcoming it is so important. Foremost, you want to put yourself in position to make some pivotal moves once you are out of school. Therefore, you must make some choices now that will lay that foundation. For all students—even the best athletes—academics is a non-negotiable contributor to success. Therefore, you must have it! My hope is that by reading this book your perspective is being broadened for how you can use school as a resource. For a moment, let's disregard how you feel about school, good or bad. Bottom line, if you are reading this book then you are likely in school; therefore, you need to take advantage of how it can help you get to the next level in your life. In this regard, let's look at how your current academic performance is shaping your future.

Maybe one of your goals is to go to college. Maybe you even have the college picked out in your head and know what you want to major in. Well, have you looked up what it takes to get into that college and get a scholarship? What GPA must you have? What is the minimum ACT score required? If you haven't taken the ACT, how are you preparing for it right now? If college is something you want to pursue then these are just a few of the critical questions you must begin asking yourself to set the right academic goals to continue moving in the direction of your vision. If you don't know the answer to these questions, then it will be virtually impossible to set goals that you are motivated to achieve. Nonetheless, even if you do not aspire to go to college after graduation, academic goals are integral to developing the skills that will help you get to wherever you want to go.

Goal-setting

I want to share a quick story with you. My sophomore year of high school was probably the apex of my laziness curve. That year I took a business typing class that I wasn't thrilled about taking. My sole motivation for getting my work done was the fact that every assignment was timed, and the teacher constantly walked around the classroom monitoring students. As a result, by the end of the semester I had developed the skills that were expected to be attained during the class. Unfortunately, that wasn't all tha was needed to get the desired result. Naturally, I wanted to get an "A" out of the class—it was an elective! However, I had not set any boundaries for myself to hold me to that standard—I had never set a goal to get an "A" in the class. My teacher had only taken up work periodically throughout the semester, so at the end I still had most of the work I had completed in my bookbag. When my teacher finally asked for it, I didn't want to make the effort to sort through my book bag to retrieve it to turn in. As a result, I got an "F" out of a class I should have gotten an "A" in! While I didn't have to repeat the class because it was an elective, it still affected my GPA and was a blot on my transcript. Furthermore, I got berated by my dad who couldn't understand how I got an "F". I couldn't blame him for being mad, and I was too ashamed to explain to him how it happened. All I could muster out in a nervous response was, "It was just an elective."

So, why is that story important? Well, if I had set better academic goals for myself, I would have never allowed myself to be so indifferent about my grade. It's not that I didn't want an "A". Who wouldn't want an "A" if they had the choice between that and an "F"? The bottom line is that I did not have a mindset to build for my future. Therefore, I did not set a goal for myself, and, because of that, I chose to do something that I later regretted. Before that point, I had many opportunities to set boundaries that would have helped me to have a better outcome. I knew that it wasn't a good idea to just shove my papers into my bookbag wherever they would fit. I could have taken 5 minutes to create a section in my bookbag to organize my assignments! However, because I didn't set a goal, in one moment of negligence I forgot why turning in those assignments was important. While it felt burdensome at that moment, my focus should have been on my grade.

Ironically, I failed what was probably my easiest class of high school. I'm sure I "paid" for that "F" in some unforeseen way, whether it was a scholarship review committee passing me over or my continued struggles with laziness through my first few years of college. More times than not, our decisions are much bigger than the moment we are in. Therefore, it is important that you make the necessary sacrifices now so that you can reap the benefits later. Furthermore, setting academic goals will help you challenge yourself and develop the stamina needed to see the vision for your life come to pass.

Endurance

Part of setting the right academic goals is focusing on the right things. I have noticed that oftentimes students are satisfied just to be performing better than their peers. They don't focus on how well they can really do, and many times they set the bar too low for themselves. One of the things that made my business typing class tolerable for me was that I enjoyed being in competition with the person next to me. I loved seeing who I could type faster than! Yet, in the end, that had little importance since I didn't pass the class. Considering my folly, remember that your most intense competitor should always be yourself. While others may think you are doing well, most importantly, you must know how well you can do and set the bar accordingly. There is no excuse for not challenging yourself to set the highest standard of academic success you believe you can achieve.

Though I am encouraging you to reach for the stars, I want to be clear on something: We live in a society that makes it easy to take the low road. Every day, students have the choice to cheat and get an easy grade or strive to learn and get the grade they deserve. Ironically, the behaviors that you set in school will translate far beyond those four walls. You must be careful with this. If your success is only about making the grade you may take any means necessary to get it, whether it is within the rules or not. On the contrary, you must remember that your academic success is about more than grades—it is about creating a better life for you and your family. You will not be in school forever. At some point, you will need the skills and character that you are supposed to be developing in school. You need to make the most of this opportunity while you can. If you are not bettering yourself then you are just "spinning your wheels."

While your classes may not always seem relevant, if you invest your time and energy in them you will be able to lay a strong foundation for your career path. This goes far beyond just getting good grades so you can get into college; if you commit to doing the best you can do then college will be one of your many options. Whether you desire to run a thriving

business by the time you graduate high school, or simply earn a full

college scholarship, the opportunity is right in front of you. As you focus

on setting academic goals, you will begin seeing school in a whole new

light and will begin to achieve in ways that you once could not imagine.

SELF-REFLECTION

52. Do you have any academic goals for the school year? If so, what are they?

53. Do you understand what it takes to accomplish your goals? Explain.

54. How are you adjusting from last school year to get the results you want?

55. Are you working with anyone (teacher, parent, principal, counselor) to make sure you reach your goals? Why or why not?

56. Rate the following subjects in order from 1-5 (1 being your favorite) based on how you feel about them:

English
Math
Science
History

Social Studies

67. Consider your highest-ranking subject (#1)? Why do you think it is your favorite?

68. Do you think that this subject complements your career interests and goals? If so, how?

69. What were your two lowest rankings (#'s 4 & 5)? What don't you like most about these subjects and why?

70. How might these subjects complement your career interests and goals?

71. What do you think your teachers can do to improve the learning experience for you in these subjects?

72. Do you think any disinterest in your least favorite subjects affects your behavior in any way? If so, how?

CHAPTER 13—CAREER GOALS

Productivity

More times than not, when I ask students about their career plans, they explain what they are "going to do" but not actually what they "are doing." So, my question to you is, "What are you doing right now to build the life you want?" Hopefully, by now, you have started developing a vision that captures both the impact you want to have on the world and the quality of life you desire for you and your family. Maybe you even know what you want to do as a career. Through this chapter, I hope to shed some light on your perspective of setting career goals and how you should work towards them.

As implied throughout this book, your interests are a strategic tool for setting the path to your vision. None of us really know how things will come together to bring our vision to pass. Therefore, we must simply set a starting point based on our interests and learn as we go. The more honest you are with yourself, the easier this process becomes. On one hand, you don't want to set goals for a career path that is completely opposite of the lifestyle you want. On the other hand, you also don't want to pursue something that does not use your talents. Again, if there is no evidence of your interests or talents (i.e., there are no noticeable patterns in your life that either you or others see), then you may need to re-evaluate your prospective career path. For instance, if an individual says that they want to be a writer but has never shown interest in writing by keeping a journal or a blog, that may be a sign that he or she should pursue an alternative career path. On the contrary, maybe he or she simply needs to set some time aside to really give writing a try. They may have some real potential that has not been tapped into due to certain circumstances.

In setting career goals, being "realistic" is highly important. For a moment, I want you to take a step outside of yourself and look at what you proclaim to perform well at, as well as what you want to do for a living. Do you really believe that? Or is it something you have said only because it feels good to say? I have had quite a few students tell me that they want to be professional athletes; however, their proclamations have not been grounded on any tangible evidence. In fact, some of these students didn't even play for their school teams! They each had some excuse for why they didn't play—the school team wasn't good, they didn't like the coach, or they were pursuing other avenues for developing and showcasing their abilities.

Earlier in the book, we discussed how a person that genuinely believes something will have a passion that causes them to take action. Those who claim to want a professional future in athletics should seek every opportunity to compete, develop their skills, and gain exposure. The reality is that only a very small percentage of high school players get a shot at playing professionally. Therefore, while it is not completely impossible to make it professionally for someone who is not competing against the best players at other schools, it is highly unlikely since they are not undergoing the process that the vast majority of professional athletes go through to make it. While it is good to aspire, those aspirations must be coupled with practicality.

Perseverance

No matter what career field you pursue, it will take hard work, commitment, and discipline to produce the results you want. Remember, there is always more to success than meets the eye. For instance, while many individuals on social media make certain career lifestyles look cool the commitment required is not always obvious. The real success that you see those few at the top have reflects many years of diligence in their crafts and the life skills that they have developed over time. You may have heard the saying, "Anything worth having is worth waiting for." Well, there is no such thing as "overnight success!" While you may experience some quick results, true success comes with time and effort.

Even a career that you think you might enjoy will take time to develop before it becomes a sustainable source of income. For instance, being a professional YouTuber has grown in popularity as a career interest for students. At first glance, it seems like an easy and fun way to make money. However, a deeper look at this reveals just how much is involved in being successful with it. One of the most challenging aspects is

"Anything worth having is worth waiting for."

building an audience. While you may have some friends that say they will support you, when it comes to growing a consistent base of followers this takes a lot of work. To make the experience engaging for your audience you will need to dedicate time to recording, video editing, and script writing. Depending on your concept, you may even need to hold a casting call for certain roles and form a production team—and let's not forget the mandatory technical aspects of setting, lighting, and sound! While a growing number of individuals have found success as YouTubers, more times than not it has been years in the making. To be successful, they have had to diligently hone their skills, constantly develop content that people want to see, and consistently market their material. It's just not as easy as it looks.

In establishing career goals, it is important to understand the work that it will take to really establish yourself in the career of your choice. Talent will only get you so far, and every career field has a certain set of skills that are needed to support that career. Therefore, while you may not know exactly what you want to do right now, you need to be aware of the "life skills" that are required for any career path you choose as well as practical approaches to career development. For instance, life skills such as budgeting and time management are common to all career fields. You will need to know how to do these things! On the other hand, there are skills that are in demand right now that can be valuable in whatever career field you choose. An example of one of these skills is computer programming. To help you better understand the preparation that goes into establishing a strong foundation for career success, we are going to briefly define and analyze gifts, talents, and skills. While these terms can be used in various ways, I will attempt to explain them in the context of both personal development and career planning.

Diligence

We briefly discussed skills and talents earlier in the book. Now we will look at how they are related to gifts. Foremost, a "gift" is a capacity that an individual is born with to function emotionally, mentally, and physically in a certain way. You may have to take a serious self-assessment to recognize your gifts. Gifts are typically broad in description. Examples of gifts are communication and creativity. All gifts must be honed to produce a desired result. That result can typically be categorized as either a "skill" or a "talent." Let's look at a simple example of the relationship between gifts, skills, and talents for the gift of being able to use your legs:

Gift	Having the use of your legs
Skill	Ability to walk or run
Talent	World-class speed

As you know, the skills of walking and running can be developed by those with the ability to use their legs. However, very few of us have world class speed. Nonetheless, while this is a talent, it still must be cultivated. For example, someone with world-class speed that never enters a race will never realize how fast they truly are. It is our variations of gifts that make us each unique. These gifts make up our personality and basic everyday functions.

We each have an opportunity to develop our gifts into skills and talents. For instance, many individuals have a gift of a sense of humor; however, few of them cultivate the talent to make others laugh. Furthermore, even fewer develop their gift into enough skill to be a standup comedian. Recognizing your gifts and determining the skills and talents you desire (and are willing) to develop is integrally important to choosing the right career. You do not want to make the mistake of spending countless hours dreaming—and even working—towards something you have very little potential to accomplish or do not genuinely want. Since we have already established how you can test your interests through setting goals, we will now look at the art of setting some career goals based on those interests.

In all practicality, your interests should match up with your talents and the skills you are willing to develop. In my experience, many students do not have a firm grasp of this concept. On one hand, students are under the impression that they should choose a career because of the demand for it in society but not necessarily because of a real interest. Many individuals that go down this path develop the skills that enable them to have a career but lack the passion or talent that would make them exceptional. On the other hand, some students choose a career based on a real interest (and talent) but don't understand that they still must develop the skills that will sustain them in that field. Therefore, they approach building a career like a hobby, not understanding that they must still perfect their craft (including the business side of it) to make a living from it.

The following example might help clarify how skills and talents accompany each other in terms of career goals. While there are many talented singers, the majority of those with aspirations of being a recording artist do not attain that goal. Besides the sheer reality that there are only so many spots available with major record labels, a huge factor in this is the reality that there is an array of underlying skills that it takes to support the talents of a successful professional artist. Artists must perfect their performance skills, hone various vocal techniques, constantly create music that audiences want to hear, and master the art of marketing themselves, just to name a few.

Planning

Your approach to career development should enable you to pursue your interests and hone both the talents and skills necessary to support your prospective career. Furthermore, it is wise to develop skills that can help you expand your value in your chosen career field as well as help you market yourself. As an example, let's use the scenario of an individual that wants to be a professional dancer. While this individual may be good at dance, if dancing was the only thing that he or she excelled in then their value would be limited to only those wanting to see them dance. However, if he or she developed the writing skills to publish a book on dancing techniques, then they would extend their value to those wanting to learn about those techniques. It is important to note that he or she would not have to be a passionate writer to do this but would simply need the skills and determination.

There is no "right" way to hone your skills and talents. Just as there are many combinations of goals that can get you to your vision, your skills and talents can be developed in many ways. For instance, some of the same skills that you might develop by majoring in Business Administration in college you might develop by working for a small business. To decide how you should go about pursuing your career, you must consider your vision as well as the minimum requirements for your chosen career interest. For instance, let's consider an individual that has a passion for helping people through the medical field. Foremost, in terms of evaluating his or her vision, that individual must determine how they see themselves in that field. Is it as a doctor? Is it a pharmacist? Or, what if that individual has a knack for organizing data? In that case, their niche might be in medical records such as in the case of a health information technician.

Figuring out what you want to focus on in your career field is an integral first step in forming a career path. To the best of your ability, you should make sure to base this on your interests, skills, and talents. From there, you can evaluate the requirements to decide if you are willing to set those goals. For instance, if you conclude that you want to be a certain type of medical doctor then you will need to evaluate if you are up to enduring that 10 to 14-year journey through college, medical school, and residency. On the other hand, if you are more interested in medical records, then you might look at working limited duties in a small medical practice right out of high school and working on a two-year degree that will unlock greater opportunities.

There are a variety of ways that an individual can approach their career interests. Therefore, in terms of strategy, only you can truly define your success. However, your strategy should be based on your vision, the goals that you set for achieving that vision, and your belief in the skills and talents that support both your vision and goals. I really want to help you understand this! Let me ask you a question: If you had the choice of making $80,000 right of high school or making it right out of college and you were able to do the type of work you wanted to do in both cases, which would you choose? I will let you think about that. This is not a trick question. The major factor in a decision like that should be how each scenario fits into your vision. Some people might view attending college right out of high school as "better." However, only you can define what is best for you. If accepting that job out of high school fits into your vision, then you should go for it! Likewise, if you see college being an integral part of your vision, then that should be the route you take.

A real-life scenario of the question I just posed is carried out every day with technology companies. While these companies value the skill sets that are often developed in college, they hold a special place for mature high school graduates that have expertise in computer programming. Therefore, a high school graduate might find a company that hires him or her right out of high school based on their skillset. Considering the demand for that skillset, that individual might earn a salary that is more than most college graduates make even 5 years out of college!

Notice that I specified that both scenarios provided an opportunity for doing what you wanted to do. In defining your success, you must be careful that you don't allow the perception of predefined standards of success to obstruct the path that is truly best for you. You will miss out on great opportunities for timely growth and development if you allow others to define success for you. You must continually determine what success looks like for you and make your decisions based on the path you want to take. To assist you, the following is a chart that shows four major work styles and how they compare to each other. There is no right or wrong answer but a matter of preference. Furthermore, this is meant to help you affirm your career interests.

Career Type	Job Market Description
Laborer	Individual can be easily replaced and has little control over work hours; requires a basic, common skill set
Employee (Low to High Level)	Individual has a moderate to highly developed skill set in a specific career field; pay is based on position/rank with minimal control of work hours
Expert/ Consultant	Individual has a highly developed skill set that the market demands; has little to moderate control of work hours and sets own pay rate (based on market demand)

CEO/ Entrepreneur	Regulates services or products that are in demand; has the general flexibility to focus time on various aspects of the business as needed or desired

There are a few things I want you to notice about the above chart. The first level, Labor, is what you can get right now—without any significant developed skills at all, you can get hired. Examples of required skills for jobs in this category might include "being able to stand for an extended period of time" or "lifting heavy objects." While it is good to know you have easy access to making money, you must also understand that this low bar of entry makes you easily replaceable.

An example of an "Entry-Level" position would be something an individual does right out of college within his or her career field. Another example might be the health information technician mentioned previously. While that individual may not need a college degree, they must be able to display an exceptional level of professionalism, attention to detail, and organization. Those who can continually develop skills that make them increasingly proficient in their career field progress to High-Level positions.

The "Consultant" level requires the drive to hone a unique set of skills that meet the market demands of a particular niche. Examples of this would be medical doctors that run their own practice, acclaimed comedians that are able to effectively market their entertainment services on a broad scale, and lawn care/landscaping companies that are able to build a steady client base; while each of these can regulate their own workload, they are still paid based on their time.

Finally, there is the "CEO" level. The CEO level warrants an exceptional combination of skills and talents. The main difference between the CEO and the Consultant is that the Consultant is paid for his or her time while the CEO makes money based on the market demand of their products and services. This is where successful YouTubers and entrepreneurs fit in; those that are most successful at this hire teams that carry the workload while they strategically spend minimal time on specific endeavors that maximize the growth of their business. The most successful entrepreneurs leverage their influence as consultants to grow their business as CEOs.

Ideally, the CEO works to improve the processes that grow their business exponentially which results in increased efficiency for his or her time and money. While the CEO level was once relegated to large brick-and-mortar companies, the advent of the internet has created a growing number of opportunities for individuals to operate at this level with little material overhead. An example of this can be seen in the burgeoning growth of the online course business which, in comparison to brick-and-mortar, requires minimal capital investment to get a business off the ground.

So, which of these categories appeal to you? When considering a career, you must keep in mind that in addition to choosing something you like, you are also choosing how you desire to make a living. Therefore, it is important to research as much as possible so you can understand what it takes to operate in your chosen career field. This starts with asking the right questions. For instance, if you have decided that you want to go to college to study a certain career field then you need to do your research on what it entails. How much money does it pay? What does the college curriculum for that major look like? What does a typical position in this career field look like on a weekly basis? Prior to choosing your career path, you should be able to reel off answers to these questions quickly and precisely.

Commitment

One of the main issues I had with my entry-level engineering position out of college was that I was sitting behind a desk for 8 hours out of the day. While that may not sound like a big deal for some people, for a vibrant 22-year-old wanting to be out front somewhere making an impact on society, that felt like punishment! On the contrary, if I had known how to establish a vision and evaluate my interests and goals, then I would not have ended up in that predicament. Let me clarify. I am not saying that pursuing engineering was a total mistake for me. I am simply saying that, even within the engineering field, understanding these things would have likely helped me to choose a scope of engineering that was more reflective of my interests and talents. To choose an ideal career position, you not only need to have a strong and valid interest in that career field, but you also need to define exactly why you want to pursue it. Does it reflect the talents you want to develop? What skills does it require? What work style do you desire?

One major benefit of evaluating your interests now is that you can begin developing the skills needed for those interests long before you have graduated from high school. For instance, if you wanted to become a doctor, now would be the time to read online medical journals and get involved with local organizations that introduce students to the medical field. Similarly, if you wanted to be a YouTuber, this would be the time to start uploading videos and building your audience. By starting now, you will see what it takes and be able to determine if you want to pursue it as a career. If you cannot passionately work on these things now, you will be hard pressed to do them later in life when you have the burden of more responsibilities. Therefore, in choosing a career field, you should also consider what you can do for the long haul.

Contrary to what it may seem, the simple acts of committing yourself to attending class and doing your schoolwork can produce a roadmap to your career. You may be asking, "How?" Well, foremost, the more you learn the more you will grasp concepts of various career fields that will improve your ability to decipher what you want to pursue. Furthermore, since schools generally offer elective courses—or at least access to various online resources that serve a similar purpose—this expands your opportunities to discover your niche. Being honest with yourself and open with your teachers and counselors about what you like, dislike, and have difficulty with will help you evaluate what might be an ideal career field and the best electives for you to take.

School is meant to serve as a foundation for helping you become a responsible and contributing member of society. Therefore, upon graduation you should have the life skills and academic skills that are necessary to make progress toward whatever you put your mind to. Yet, while this concept seems simple, many students wake up to a harsh reality after they graduate—they are not prepared for life outside those four walls! To be prepared for life after high school you need to have a realistic perspective of your prospective career path and how school can both guide and prepare you. Whether you realize it or not, any career field you choose will have a direct relationship with at least one of your core subjects. Knowing this relationship can help you gauge your real interests. The following table is an example of some relationships between high school curriculums and several popular career fields.

Career Field	Most Relevant High School Core Subjects	Relevant High School Electives
Nursing	Biology, Anatomy	Food & Nutrition, Early Childhood Development
Engineering	Calculus, Physics	Urban Planning, Computer Programming
Lawyer	State and Local Government, Civics	Policy & Law, Debate

Accountant	Algebra I, Algebra II	Finance, Business Management
Actor	Language Arts, History	Theatre, Stage Production

Remember, it is your responsibility to lay a solid foundation! Research your interests and ask your guidance counselors to help you based on what you discover. Consider electives that might help you learn more about your interests and help you evaluate them. Ask yourself, what makes those classes more beneficial to you than other classes? There are a variety of electives and online resources that relate to any given career field. If you find that you are not interested in anything that relates to one of your career interests, then you may want to re-evaluate that interest.

While you may not like some core subjects, it is important that you consider why you feel that way. Your courses have the potential to give life to your ideas and desires. Therefore, when considering your core subjects, your perspective can be broadened by viewing them through the lens of what you are interested in. For instance, if you are interested in engineering then, practically speaking, you should have a natural enjoyment for math and science. If that is not the case, then you would likely need to evaluate why you feel the way you do and make a logical decision about pursuing that career interest. Remember, choosing a career field should be about finding what best fits your interests and talents, as well as determining the skills you are willing to develop.

Humility

I am going to issue you a challenge. To help you in the process of determining your career field, I recommend that you ask your supporters—those real friends that you have identified— to give you their opinion about your career goals. While no one can truly measure your full potential, your supporters have recognized your talents and can give you an unbiased opinion about what you say you want to do. Choosing the right career path is no time to shy away from constructive criticism. Since your supporters have your best interest in mind, it is important that you are not afraid of what they have to say and that you learn to look at it as objectively as possible. Extract the truth from it, adjust where needed, and go build the life you want!

As I mentioned before, you must be honest with yourself. We all have different talents. That is one of the things that makes each of us unique. If you have not already done so, you must start embracing what you have so that you can be the best possible version of yourself. If you continue to pursue your vision through managing responsibilities, executing goals, and committing to self-improvement then you are on your way to a lifetime of success.

SELF-REFLECTION

73. What are your top 3 career interests right now? Explain why you are interested in each one.

74. What subjects are your career interests most related to?

75. What electives are you considering taking that relate to your career interests? Name at least three. If you don't know the exact name, come up with a creative title that might relate.

76. What steps will you take to work towards your career at school and away from school?

CHAPTER 14—PLANNING

Planning

What is the use of knowing what you want—and even believing you can achieve it—if you never act on it? Earlier in the book we discussed how true belief leads to action. Well, there is one very glaring exception to this rule: Even if you are compelled to act, a lack of planning will lead to inaction. Have you ever heard the saying, "If you fail to plan then you plan to fail?" Many individual's ideas never leave their head! Why do you think that is? While fear and extenuating circumstances have a part to play, much of this inaction can be attributed to a lack of planning.

By now you have heard a spiel or two about the importance of planning. Even if you have not heard it formally, you've gotten it in the form of people asking you questions like: "What are your plans after high school?" "What college are you going to?" "What will you major in?" While you may not know exactly what you want to do or how it will pan out, you should always actively be preparing for your future.

"If you fail to plan, then you plan to fail."

Ironically enough, many students get to graduation and realize that the one thing they have not done effectively is plan. While they have aspired, they have not planned!

So, now we will talk about planning. One indispensable factor of a plan is that it must be written down and organized. Only then can you really begin to strategize for your future. Having a plan will help you stay prepared to endure the process of achieving what you want. Many students do not have a plan upon graduation because up until that point they have not had to have one. Think about it: In middle and high school your tasks are spelled out for you—you must attend class, study for tests, complete homework, etc. If you continue to do those things then graduation will come. There is not much planning required on your part to graduate. Unfortunately, however, for many students there are no clear-cut next steps after graduation. Therefore, you must begin to consider that the clock for your future has already started ticking. That clock will seem to tick even faster after graduation. Since you will not have the structure you had in high school, you will need a plan to ensure that you continue to make progress. No matter what path you choose upon graduation—whether the military, college, or the workforce—having a plan will enable you to uphold your responsibilities and take advantage of the opportunities presented to you.

You can never start planning too early. If you have not already started, this is your opportunity. Now, we will break down how a plan works so that you can understand the importance of it for yourself. Foremost, a plan is a framework for implementing your goals into your daily life—that is, it is your instruction manual for getting from "Point A" to "Point B". Your plan considers everything we have discussed so far—interests, goals, responsibilities, responses to positive and negative influences, etc. However, we will simplify planning by elaborating a few themes emphasized throughout this book: Establishing a Vision, Implementing Goals, and Setting Boundaries.

As a refresher, we will now revisit our definitions of vision, goals, and boundaries. We defined vision as "knowing what you want out of life."

We defined goals as "the steps you take to get to your vision." Finally, we defined boundaries as "rules that you put in place to help you accomplish your goals." Each of these should contribute to ensuring that your ideas become actions. As alluded to earlier in the book, acting is the only way you will ever make progress towards your vision. It is the glue that brings everything together. Many times, by committing yourself to taking specific actions, those actions serve as boundaries that ensure your progress. Furthermore, as you develop more understanding for how each action affects the desired outcome you will be able to better plan your actions for making progress.

Ensuring that your vision, goals, and boundaries align is key to effective planning. Ideally, your plan should help you evaluate if you are spending time on the right things. To begin our analysis of planning, we will analyze the differences between the plans of a student upon entering his or her freshmen and senior years of high school. We will assume that this student already knows that they want to be a social worker and has known it for a while.

Entering Freshman Year

Vision	Attend college for social work on an academic or athletic scholarship
Goals	Get A/B Honor Roll
	Make the school basketball team
Boundaries (Planned Actions)	Limit the time I spend watching television and on social media
	Increase homework and study time
	Meet with my teachers on a regular basis to check on my grades
	Practice basketball for two hours per day in preparation for tryouts

We see from the table that this student's goals support his or her vision. We also see that these boundaries (planned actions) are meant to help him or her accomplish their goals. When you are planning, it is important that you are as specific as possible with your boundaries so that it will be as practical as possible to follow through with them. In our example, it is not hard to see how these boundaries can become a part of this student's weekly routine. In fact, if this student is to be successful with his or her goals, it is imperative that this happens.

Now we will look at what a plan might look like for this same student entering his or her senior year.

Entering Senior Year

Vision	In 5 years, I will work as a social worker living in the Washington D.C. area
Goals	I will maintain a 3.5 GPA
	In 1 month, I will take the ACT
	In 3 months, I will take the ACT to improve my score
	In 5 months, I will get accepted into a college of my choice

	In 7 months, I will know how I will pay for my first year of college
	In 5 years, I will graduate college with the honor of magna cum laude
Boundaries (Planned Actions)	Designate 2 hours per day to schoolwork
	Study for ACT at least 10 hours per week
	Fill out applications for 10 colleges
	Apply for at least 3 scholarships per week
	Collect recommendations for college applications from family and school staff

As you may have noticed in comparing the two plans, the plan for this individual's senior year is significantly more detailed. While the visions are similar, the goals entering senior year become much more time-oriented because they must meet approaching deadlines and specific requirements that were not as relevant a few years earlier. Much like the plan of this student evolved from his or her first year to their last year, those that want to continue making progress after high school toward their vision must continue to evolve by honing their interests and establishing more definitive goals.

A plan will help you continue to define your vision as you begin to learn more about yourself. Understanding the concept of planning is extremely important to you developing a practical approach to establishing a career and experiencing long-term success. The planning process never stops. As you and your circumstances evolve, your plans will evolve. This is a product of actively evaluating results and making modifications to improve those results. Therefore, your main objective in planning should be to establish a system that works for you. Once you develop that skill, you will be able to use it for the rest of your life. As you continue to plan you will be able to constantly evaluate the validity of your ideas, set more definitive goals, and optimize the steps you take to accomplish those goals.

Goal setting

Earlier in this book, we discussed how executing goals can help you test your interests and either bring you closer to your vision or help you realize that you need to re-evaluate it. In the same way, executing your plan will help you establish the right goals. This is a process. Consider this analogy: Very seldom does any inventor get the design for his or her invention right the first time. Many times, it takes tens and even hundreds of iterations before they get a working model. While the inventor may have had the same goal in mind each time before, the previous designs did not serve their intended function. In the same way, a plan is only as good as how effective it is in helping you make progress. You will know that you have a good planning process when you are able to consistently use what you learn about yourself to develop more relevant and concise goals, complete tasks, and make daily adjustments to ensure you stay productive.

As we have discussed throughout this book, it is integral that your goals align with your vision. You may remember the story I told earlier about my struggles in college due to a lack of vision. Well, I experienced similar struggles with writing my first book. Before I published it, I had started the process of writing that book at least eight times, each time with the goal of completing it. The pattern was the same every time: I would get excited about writing and would establish a grandiose illusion in my head that I could finish it in a month or so; then by the second week I would be so discouraged at my seeming lack of progress that I would just stop writing. While I had the desire, I did not have the vision!

The prior times that I had tried writing a book I had simply been writing because I had a desire to write a book. It was a nice idea, but it did not yet fit into the "big picture" for my life and, therefore, did not motivate me enough to continue writing through the tough moments. In the same way, if you do not establish a firm vision, then it will be almost impossible for you to endure (and enjoy) the process of achieving the goals you set. It was not until I had defined a clear vision for my life that I could sit and write consistently enough to complete a book. By that time, I knew what I wanted and believed that it was meant for me to achieve it.

Just as I was not successful the first eight times that I tried to write a book, some of your goals may not work the first time around. That is okay. Those goals may not be the best use of your skills and talents, or they just may not align with your vision. On the other hand, they may not encompass something you genuinely believe in. Nonetheless, if you are willing to continually assess your interests and act on your goals, you will master the art of determining the right goals to make progress towards your vision. In doing so, you will further clarify your vision.

Perseverance

Building the life you want takes time. If you find yourself pursuing something which you are not willing to build towards gradually then it is a good sign that you need to re-evaluate your motivation. You may find that it is not something you really want and that it may just be a byproduct of what you have been influenced to believe that you should have. An example of this is how I thought I wanted to be the CEO of a tech company but was not committed enough to teach myself to do the most important part! In retrospect, I see the various influences at play that blinded me from realizing that this was not the right goal for me. On the one hand, I had bought into the idea that this was the best route to prove my value as an influencer to others and, therefore, I was trying to define my place in society by that instead of who I was as a person. In addition, I had financial pressures that caused me to want to rush things. These things considered, I was operating by what I thought I needed and not necessarily by what I truly needed. My perception was off!

I want to leave you with this final analogy for planning. If you have ever done a physical workout on a regular basis, then you know that it is when you press through the pain that you get the best results. Furthermore, if you genuinely want results, it is not enough to just work out here-and-there. You must be consistent! It is the same with a plan. Consider your plan as the muscle-building regimen for your vision. When you seriously plan, it hurts. Following through with what you have professed to want (and believe) requires discipline and sometimes discomfort; however, the result will be what you want.

Right now, you may feel like you have a lot of options in life for the success you envision, and that may very well be the case. However, if you want success that lasts, then learning how to execute your plan is an indispensable tool. A plan is your roadmap and there are no shortcuts and no pots of gold at the end of any rainbows. While pipe dreams do not require a plan, real dreams do. If you did not have the knowledge prior to reading this book, you now have what you need to plan effectively. So, start planning now! I guarantee that one day you will look back and be glad you did.

SELF-REFLECTION

77. What goals do you currently have? How much time will you spend every week on each one?

78. How will you avoid peer pressure to reach your goals?

79. How will you utilize your support system to reach your goals?

CHAPTER 15—AFFIRMATION

Courage

You may have noticed a recurring emphasis throughout this book on the importance of being honest with yourself. In the process of growth and development, this is an indispensable element. Without it you will inevitably live a life that—while it may appear successful to others—is a disappointment to your potential. In fact, many people go in the opposite direction of what they genuinely want because they are not honest with the reality of their circumstances. Therefore, they cannot take the necessary steps to continue moving in the direction of their vision. While establishing a vision is the most important thing you can do at this moment, to do so you must be honest with yourself. Once that is established, you can begin assessing what needs to be done and can then act accordingly.

Let me make it clear that there will be obstacles on the path to developing the life you want. Those obstacles will come in many shapes and sizes. Some will be self-inflicted, some will be brought on by others, and some may seem to happen for no rhyme or reason. Yet, they all can be overcome! If you keep taking actions that align with your vision, you will eventually get there. However, to do this you must begin planning to overcome adversity. Now we will delve a little into what this adversity might look like so that you will be able to identify it.

As I mentioned in the first chapter, years down the road when you look back on your life anything that may have stopped you from accomplishing your vision will seem small. Your perspective of life will evolve, and you will be able to see that the reasons for compromising what you wanted were not worth it. None of us will do everything perfectly, but we can actively minimize the potential for regret. The obstacles that you face now, and will face soon, will only seem relevant to you if you are being honest with yourself. Let me explain. The reality is, we all have the power to make up in our minds that something is not what it truly is. You have the power to forfeit what you genuinely want by telling yourself you do not want it and making excuses for why you do not go after it. That is called self-deception. Many people start this pattern early on in life, and it is fortified over time through habit. This is one of the ways many individuals become their own worst enemy. You have the opportunity right now to combat this tendency by recognizing its existence.

So, why would anyone deceive themselves? The logic behind this is quite simple. None of us want to fail! When we are faced with failure, it is often easier to convince ourselves that we either do not care about the results or that the outcome can still be what we want even if we do not take the necessary steps. That is just not how it works! Everything you want in life will have steps that are required. However, it is your responsibility to acknowledge (and accept) when it is time to take those steps. On your road to personal success, your biggest obstacle to progress will be the fear of failure. I have told students in the past like this, "No matter what you really want, fear is the obstacle you will have to overcome." Fear will always be in opposition to your vision, belief, and goals. If you allow it to, it will keep you from taking action.

So, how do we combat fear? There are a couple popular acronyms for fear, but one that I heard years ago captures what I believe is important for you to understand right now: Fear stands for "False Expectations Appearing Real." Notice the word "expectation." How we approach things typically depends on what we expect the outcome to be. Therefore, we tend to shy away from outcomes that we see as negative. Fear is a "false expectation" because it emphasizes the potential for an undesired outcome in lieu of one that is desired. That is, while you may believe you can have what you want, fear tells you that you cannot have it. Many individuals allow their fear to become their reality because they become attached to the possibility of an undesired outcome. The irony in this is that none of us can control our outcomes! As soon as you are more concerned with controlling the outcome than you are about controlling your actions, you will be stopped in your tracks. The better you can relinquish the perception that you can control the outcome of your actions the easier it will be to face your fears.

For every affirming belief you have, there is the potential to have doubts that challenge that belief. If you allow yourself to focus on those doubts, then you will not move forward. That is fear! Yet, if you stay focused on your actions instead of worrying about what will happen, then you will continue making progress. Therefore, your power rests in your ability to control your actions. While fear many times reflects a possible outcome, you must remember that, when you are focused on your vision, every failure and shortcoming can be viewed as something to be learned from and built upon. That is the perspective you must have if you want to experience ongoing personal success. Furthermore, if you define your standard of success by the progress you can make within yourself —and not by what others have defined as success— then you can never really fail.

Resilience

Now that we have looked at fear, we will look at how it can be perpetuated by wrong beliefs. It can be painful to accept that there are some things about our lives that we have "missed the mark" on. We all have had shortcomings that we are not fond of and that may have left unpleasant memories. Many times, we let those experiences haunt us and hold us hostage with the fear of them happening again. As we discussed with negative influences earlier in the book, there are many things we experience that form our beliefs about ourselves. Yet, many of those beliefs are just not true!

There were things that happened to me in high school that plagued me long into my professional life. Every time I would begin to see myself better than how I saw myself in the past, thoughts of the past would come to my mind that would try to tell me I could never be different than that person I used to feel like. I had to finally determine within myself that those things would not define me! When I did, I was able to embrace my present and future wholeheartedly and I was able to silence that voice. On your road to success, you must determine that you will not be defined by your past shortcomings. Let the past be the past! While I know that is easier said than done, it can be done! The more you embrace this mentality, the freer you will become to pursue your vision.

Only you have the power to validate your vision and, thereby, take the necessary actions to overcome adversity. Consider this metaphor: One morning I woke up with an image in my head of a lion that had constantly backed up in cowardice as another lion growled. It backed up until it was cornered and could not go any further. Then I heard the words, "At some point you have to growl back." Though I did not see the full picture, I knew that the once fearful lion began to growl back and, as it did, the other lion began to slowly step back. The thing that stood out to me most about that whole scene was that the lion that was backing up at first was acting out of character. It was still a lion! That observation alone told me all that I needed to know—that lion did not truly embrace its identity until it growled back.

In life, at some point you will have to growl back. Therefore, you must determine the things that are truly important to you. What is it that you want? What have you identified that makes you uniquely suited to accomplish it? Do you believe that you can achieve it? The answers to these questions hold the blueprint to who you are right now and who you are meant to be. So, if you feel like you have been backed up like that lion in any place in your life, you must first realize that the real culprit is not the obstacle in front of you but, instead, is fear. You must acknowledge and embrace who you are and who you are meant to be through your thoughts, words, and deeds. Once you do that, your environment will begin to change. That is how you growl back!

Endurance

On your journey of personal success there will be naysayers along the way, and there will be people that tell you it cannot be done; however, I want to encourage you to use that as constructive criticism and fuel to keep going. While you know what you have inside, it will take time for others to see it. Even then, some people will not want to see it. Regardless of people's scrutiny, you must embrace self-contentment and work to do what you know is right for you. If you continue to build on that foundation, there will come a time when it yields a product that everyone will see. At that point, you will be walking in the manifestation of your vision and will have developed the character necessary to sustain your success.

The pursuit of what you genuinely want is a continuous process. Contrary to what it may seem, it is okay to not be quite certain of what you want—vision is developed through the planning and execution of goals. Nonetheless, if you do not manage your time well enough to follow through on your goals then there is a good chance that you will lose sight of your vision. It is not that you will not still have a desire for the same things, but you may lose the sense of urgency that is needed to make meaningful decisions that will help you accomplish them.

On the road to personal success, it is the willingness to get back up again and move forward despite what your circumstances may look like that will allow you to find the hope needed to keep striving to make progress. There is no uncomplicated way of approaching this. We all have our own battles to fight, and none of us can look to the next person to fight them for us. You must learn how to overcome that adversity. The reality is that you will have to meet some of those things head on. At some point, you will have to stare fear in its face and say, "I am not allowing you to steal what I know is for me!" If you are willing to do this and follow it up with action, then you will be able to continually evolve in your progression.

In this life there are no guarantees that any accomplishment or credential will open the doors that you want it to. After earning a degree in engineering and working 8 years in that field, at one point in time circumstances still found me working what many would consider to be menial jobs, some of which I only made minimum wage. Nonetheless, there was something to be learned with each stop that helped me build towards my vision. Looking back, I can really see how each one played an integral role in my progress. Thankfully, I kept an open mind and was able to consciously embrace those opportunities. I encourage you to look at every experience as an opportunity to better yourself in your journey of personal success. If you ever find yourself feeling like you are ready to go to the next level but just do not have the opportunity, then you are not truly ready! When you are ready, the opportunity will present itself. In fact, you will make the opportunity! That is what happened to me as I began to believe in my gifts.

I had known for years, starting early on in college, that I enjoyed motivating students. When I graduated college and began working in engineering, that became something that I longed to do. I would sit up in my apartment fantasizing about standing in front of large crowds and delivering inspirational speeches. I would practice in front of the mirror. I even did research on what it took to do something like that as a career. Yet, I lacked the belief needed to take that step. I felt like I needed to be the CEO of a major company to be deemed worthy of being heard. Years later, after experiencing success with public speaking and my career, I finally got up the gumption to approach schools. To start, I presented a concept for an entrepreneurship program to a high school and began to teach it through its career readiness program. The rest is history! I continued to embrace speaking opportunities and got immersed in the classroom experience. While it was a process of a few years before I really found my niche, by taking that leap I set the stage to manifest my longtime vision of impacting students in a major way.

Ironically, when I was sitting in my apartment with what seemed like a deep unfulfilled desire, many times I felt like I just needed an opportunity to open for me. Yet, all along that opportunity was waiting for me to have the boldness to embrace it. At that time, while I knew I was a gifted communicator, I still struggled with the fear of failure. Furthermore, while I knew that I was supposed to be motivating students, that fear still outweighed my belief. I had not yet had enough experience under my belt to give me the confidence to sustain regular speaking engagements. During that time of my life, in the rare cases that I did get in front of a microphone, I got flustered. I even dreaded the idea of being on the phone with a stranger to the point that I stumbled over my words when I was paying my bills over the phone! There was still much that needed to happen in my journey before I could see my vision come to fruition.

Diligence

When I moved to Montgomery, Alabama, to take my first engineering job out of college, I already had a passion for theatre arts and public speaking. Instead of just sitting on my desire, I joined a speaking organization in which I was able to build my skills and confidence. Not long after joining that organization, I auditioned for a short film that was being produced locally. From there, I got a small role and was then invited to audition for the dramatic guild with the renowned Alabama State University Theatre Department. It was there that I overcome a panic attack in route to a successful audition which led to many acting endeavors that have helped shape my journey.

These endeavors were not easy at the time. Each one was a moment of growth. They challenged me to become a better version of myself. As I continued to put myself in positions to develop my talents and skills, I got better. Though there were some moments that I shied away from, I continued to seize opportunities that helped me make progress. In your journey of personal success, you will make some decisions that you look back on and realize that there was a better way—that's part of being human. However, when you are committed to pursuing your vision, you will have the opportunity to bridge the gaps of what you have missed along the way while utilizing the best of what you have gained. That is what happened in my case with engineering.

When I was sitting behind that desk at my first job, I was discontented. I had lacked vision, and this was the first time that I was truly faced with the reality that I was lying in the bed that I had made. Nonetheless, I eventually found contentment in doing my job well, and this led me to develop some skillsets that were not a part of my job requirements but, instead, were a product of me looking for ways to help my organization. While pursuing Broadcast Journalism would likely have been a more fulfilling endeavor, engineering has played a critical role in my professional journey. Foremost, it has helped me develop a valuable analytical skill set that I have been able to use to develop business ideas that are aligned with my vision for empowering individuals and communities. Furthermore, I have been able to couple those skills with my talents as a writer, speaker, and performer to deliver information in a highly effective way.

As you journey through life, you should try to always do your best with the opportunities you are given. While you do not know where those opportunities will lead, you can always prepare for the future by doing what you know you are supposed to do. Integrity is key! The times that I have lost sight of integrity have been the times that I have made costly decisions that have set me (and my family) back. Thankfully, I am still alive today to apply what I have learned from my mistakes.

Persistence

When I watch the news or skim online news headlines, I am constantly reminded how fleeting life can be. There is always some unforeseen event that has taken the lives of victims who, just like you and I, once aspired to do great things. Have you ever heard the saying, "The future isn't promised?" Well, I like to take that a little further and say, "The future

"The future is not promised."

isn't promised, even to those with a promising future." It is easy to look at some people and say, "Man, they are going to be somebody!" However, the reality is that none of us know when we will take our last breath. No matter how gifted, or privileged, or nice, nothing is guaranteed.

Hopefully, by now, you have embraced that being alive is a precious opportunity that is not to be wasted. While it is easy to adopt the mentality that you have plenty of time to get it right, the reality is that tomorrow may never come. However, if you have become more motivated through the course of reading this book, then that reality should invoke a greater sense of urgency for you to make the most of each day.

I have found that life looks different when we approach it like each day could be our last. While some individuals might use that as an excuse to live frivolously for the moment, wise individuals use it to prepare for tomorrow as if it were coming so that they are ready if it does come. These are the people that experience consistent personal success in life.

Every day is an opportunity for you to embrace who you were born to be! Therefore, I encourage you to start tackling the small things that you know you need to deal with today. Maybe it is a habit you do not like, or maybe it is the people you surround yourself with that you need to change. Only you know the answer, and only you can make the decision to do better.

What I have learned, through both my mistakes and triumphs, is what I have delivered to you in this book. No matter where you are or what you have done in the past, you can choose to take control of your life right now. In fact, it is your willingness to get back up again and move forward—despite what your circumstances may look like—that will allow you to establish the momentum to keep moving forward. Hopefully this book has helped you build a foundation for the rest of your life and has empowered you to choose the direction you want to go. But the ball is in your court now, and I challenge you to use everything you have read, reflected on, and discussed to aggressively move in the direction of your vision. Now that you are better equipped for your journey, the only question left is, "What will you do?"

SELF-REFLECTION

80. What do you envision yourself doing in each of the following time spans from now? (Be as detailed as possible.)

1 year?

3 years?

5 years?

APPENDIX

Definitions

The following definitions are in the context of how they are used throughout the book.

Boundary – Any constraint or guideline (e.g. a set time allotment or series of actions) established to help an individual stay on course to accomplish a goal

Gift – A capacity that an individual is born with to perform various functions, be it emotionally, mentally, or physically; a gift can be developed into skills and talents

Goal – A standard of accomplishment that one sets to build towards a vision or objective; time-oriented steps with measurable results

Objective – A desired outcome or idea that can typically be attained through the strategic execution of a series of actions or goals

Plan – A framework written or typed out that incorporates a person's goals into their daily life and assists them in measuring progress and staying on course

Purpose – A counterintuitive sense of meaning and intent that is typically related to one's vision, goals, talents, and skills

Skill – An attribute that is commonly identifiable as something that can be used to produce a desired result; the value of a skill is typically controlled by market demand

Success – The manifestation of one's vision, goals, and desires

Talent – A knack for executing an action or behavior exceptionally above average

Vision – An active consciousness of one's desires and the internalization of those desires; the state of knowing what one wants out of life in terms of career, achievements, family, quality of life, etc.

About the Author

Derek J. Lovett is an educator and motivational speaker with over 20 years of experience serving the youth in various roles including after-school enrichment programs, athletics, and public education. While teaching in the classroom one of his most glaring observations was that many of his students were reluctant to perform some of the most routine classroom procedures. In response to this, he began focusing his efforts on deciphering the systemic issues that contributed to student underperformance. Ensuing, he began writing *80 Questions for Adolescents* as a tool to assist schools and parents in better engaging students in the learning process.

In *80 Questions for Adolescents*, Derek uses a combination of compelling narratives, anecdotes, and diagrams to immerse students in the indispensable process of self-discovery. In doing so, students are motivated to learn, and those that serve them are empowered to teach.